Inheritance in Islam

European University Studies

Europäische Hochschulschriften
Publications Universitaires Européennes

Series XXVII
Asian and African Studies

Reihe XXVII Série XXVII
Asiatische und Afrikanische Studien
Etudes asiatiques et africaines

Vol./Bd. 69

PETER LANG
Frankfurt am Main · Berlin · Bern · New York · Paris · Wien

Annelies Glander

Inheritance in Islam

Women's Inheritance in Sana'a (Republic of Yemen)

Law, Religion, and Reality

PETER LANG
Europäischer Verlag der Wissenschaften

Die Deutsche Bibliothek - CIP-Einheitsaufnahme

Glander, Annelies:

Inheritance in Islam : Women's inheritance in Sana'a (Republic of Yemen) ; law, religion, and reality / Annelies Glander. - Frankfurt am Main ; Berlin ; Bern ; New York ; Paris ; Wien : Lang, 1998
(European university studies : Ser. 27, Asian and African Studies ; Vol. 69)
ISBN 3-631-34080-X

ISSN 0721-3581
ISBN 3-631-34080-X
US-ISBN 0-8204-3570-8

Printed in Germany 1 2 3 4 5 7

Acknowledgements

The author wishes to thank all those who contributed and helped her
to research, compile and present this study:
the generous and outspoken women who housed her,
the patient and benevolent imams, qadis, and other experts,
the model officials,
both those who issued permits and visas at shortest possible notice,
and those who did not request the impossible,
the co-operative librarians,
and the indefatigable informants.

And, finally, two ladies whose hearts went out to such an extent that the one made sure that the entire text was closely examined for flaws and ambiguities while the other, in genuine Arabian magnanimity, bore the cost of publication.

Table of Contents

1. Conceptual parameters

"I study life by being close to it, this 'native life' about which so little is known, and which is disfigured by the descriptions of those who, not knowing it, insist on describing it anyway ..." (Isabelle Eberhardt)[1]

1.1 A note on the state of research

"For a very long time, virtually all that was known of the Arab World had been passed on by Western travellers, whose baggage, unlike that of the native Arabs, was very heavy, especially in cultural prejudice. And if the comments passed on rang favourably, they had been romanticised by guests who had indulged in sharing hard life for a certain time and could always go back home."[2] The Western travellers could and did rely on help and faithful assistance and took everything for granted because – in line with their philosophy and upbringing – they paid what for them was comparatively little. For the native Arabs the remuneration could make all the difference in their daily living.

Considering the long years of practical experience of development aid volunteers, the ever greater accessibility of the most remote regions, the possibilities, especially for young people, to travel the world at little cost, and the numerous development projects realised, one could expect that more understanding should in the meantime have reached the bearers and opinion leaders of Western civilisation; that eventually the expeditions of social anthropologists and, foremost, the projects undertaken by field researchers could have established a new approach, might have helped to form a new attitude towards the people in Arab and Muslim countries.

---

1 Eberhardt, Isabelle: Letter to the Editor of "La Petite Gironde", Annex in: "The Oblivion Searchers", 1978:87

2 Thesiger, Wilfred: Travel through the Empty Quarter, 1959: Introduction

The author, son of a British diplomat stationed in Africa and born there, was able to fulfil his dream and go to the Arabian desert, shared life with the "**badw**" (bedouins) and exquisitely recorded hardship and adventure on the Arab peninsula. His ideas and impressions, even if admittedly personal and not intended for ethnographic documentation, present the reader with genuine, first-hand descriptions and may serve as a superb basis for individual objectivation.

With but very few exceptions, the resulting studies and reports very often indulge in pointing out differences, but fail to determine the angle of perspective.[3] More regrettably still, the authors strive to collect data to fit into their pre-established scheme, they look for confirmation of a theory established at a desk back home. And when in the field they closely study the subject the way one looks at fish in an aquarium – without getting wet. However, the now imperative request for unlimited exploration in the field may be seen as a fairly recent development and some more time may be necessary before the desired results will be available.

Nigel Barley[4], now at the Museum of Mankind in London, postulates the necessity of a sociological approach by stating that the difference between sociologists and social anthropologists is not a question of subject matter, it simply lies in their different fields of practical action, which for the one is at home, for the other on foreign territory, both geographically and culturally. And he resumes that any form of civilisation can indeed only be established by studying another civilisation.

East and West have much more in common than meets the eye at a first glance. The differences that exist between Muslim and Christian attitudes are historical, they are not absolute. Take the segregation of sexes and the closeting of women behind veils and shut doors. This tradition still continues in the East and is unquestionably out of step with present-day practice in the West. However, the concept on which this segregation is based – that women should be protected – is by no means alien to the West. And the idea of family honour and the need to safeguard it – another reason why women's liberty is curtailed – was a principle firmly upheld also in many parts of Europe, especially in the South, until relatively recent times.

There is a form of Islamic puritanism very similar to the Victorian puritanism lingering on in England: strict about religious observance, moralistic, prudish in sexual matters, disapproving of pleasure.[5]

There are still a number of exclusive clubs in London where females are only admitted if accompanied by a male. And even then the female guest will be expected to have her tea in the ladies' drawing room and not to sit in the men's lounge. Yet, would anyone refer to England as an uncivilised country?

---

3 Beck, L. & Keddie, N.: Women in the Muslim World, 1978: Introduction

4 Quoted from an article published in the weekly supplement to "Die Presse" on 5/6/1993

5 Graham, Helga: Arabian Time Machine, 1978:156–158

Carsten Niebuhr offers the following statement:

"The Europeans are mistaken in thinking the state of marriage so different among the Muslims from what it is with Christian Nations. I could not discern any such difference in Arabia. Polygamy is permitted indeed among Mahomedans, and the delicacy of our ladies is shocked at this idea; but the Arabians rarely avail themselves of the privilege of marrying four lawful wives, and entertaining at the same time any number of female slaves. None but rich voluptuaries marry so many wives, and their conduct is blamed by all sober men. Men of sense, indeed, think this privilege rather troublesome than convenient. A husband is, by law, obliged to treat his wives suitable to their condition, and to dispense his favours among them with perfect equality: but these are duties not a little disagreeable to most Muslims; and such modes of luxury are too expensive to the Arabians, who are seldom in easy circumstances."[6]

1.2 Methodology of the study

The question as to the methodology of the study undertaken cannot be answered along conventional lines. In the absence of specific documentation the *modus operandi* could not be tailored to any established pattern but was initiated by

a) the search for additional sources of information in the light of insufficient documented material and no established empirical model, and

b) the attempt to accommodate to any situation encountered in the field with as much flexibility as was considered conceivable to achieve the purpose of the investigation. The originally carefully prepared strategy of collecting information in conventional, academic routine style had ever and again to be adapted on the spur of the moment.

1.3 The Ten Commandments of Field Research

The Guidelines followed in field research by the author of the text are given in the form of the

---

6 Niebuhr, Carsten: Travel to Arabia, 1773
in: Graham, Helga: Arabian Time Machine, 1978:214

Ten Commandments of Field Research,

the first four of which are a slightly rephrased version of Freya Stark's[7] "Decalogue for Travel", quoted upon successful testing and in tribute to her, and supplemented by six more voiced on the basis of experience gained in the 1990s:

- Thou shalt be capable of accepting values and of judging by standards other than thy own and thy mind be leisurely and uncensorious.

- Thou shalt be aware that rapid judgment of the other's character and sincerity are a prerequisite for any sound investigation. Thou must proffer a ready quickness in repartee or thy opposite will rusefully give wrong answers.

- Thou must love nature and this must include human nature; thou must have a tolerable constitution and the capacity to eat and sleep at any moment.

- Thou must bring with thee a fair knowledge of local history, economic conditions, political aspects and of the language.

- Thou mayest go native but thou shalt not get carried away. Thou shalt adapt to the local surroundings but remain thyself. If thou integratest into thy field of research to such an extent that thou becomest a stranger in thy own world thou hast gone too far.

- Thou must bear in mind that thou art a guest. Thou must not interfere with circumstances, neither pity nor envy thy hosts. Thy order is to collect facts, and if thou art explicitly asked for thy opinion try to find comparable aspects in thy home country which thou canst offer.

- Thou shalt never refuse an informant – less so if he or she be introduced by one thou hast chosen thyself, no matter how negligible the outcome may be. A turned-down informant causeth unnecessary problems.

- Thou shalt not invent or misrepresent details about thyself. Thou must not introduce a chance visiting friend or lover as thy husband or beloved brother. And thou must never make advances to a native out of curiosity or on the pretext of obtaining genuine information more directly. An informant cajoled on false promises and turned down may become a dangerous enemy.

---

7 Freya Stark: Winter in Arabia, 1973

- Thou shalt be frank and modest. Thou shalt tell thy informants that thou art not familiar with their code of conduct but ready to learn. Ask them to help thee behave inoffensively and according to their expectations. And beg them, instead of giving a fake answer, to candidly tell thee if a question thou raisest inconveniences them.

- Thou shalt not expect the people back home to understand or believe thee. If thou art not prepared to be considered an outsider and suspected of highly unbecoming aspirations thou art well-advised to stay at home with the crowd and uphold the popular mind.

1.4 Possibilities of approach

Field work and research on women's issues undertaken by women is a fairly recent development. Even more recent are the contributions by Arab women.[8] One could have hoped that, once women were given access to this field of studies, a revolution in social anthropology might have taken place, followed by yet another upsurge of revelations once Arab women were admitted. As this does not seem to be the case, there must be substantial obstacles and it would seem appropriate to undertake an analysis:

Women researchers do not meet with certain obstacles experienced and referred to in anthropological studies undertaken by men: the problem of access to women[9] and the specific inter-female conversation pattern. To study and speak a language is one aspect, to understand how women express themselves, yet another. Women have a language of their own, and they express themselves differently when being together with women. And the attitude of a woman in the presence of her husband or other male members of the family will be altogether different from her behaviour with other women, or under other social circumstances.[10] The successful male researcher, having established close contact with a male and having been admitted to his house, might well be given permission to meet the wife and speak to her in the presence of her husband. The wife will politely and beautifully answer all the questions asked, knowing very well what her husband would like her to say. The

---

8 Altorki, Soraya and El Solh, Camillia Fawzi: Women in the Arab World, 1988: Introductory chapter on "Arab Women in the Field"

9 Kielstra, Niko: in Gellner, E.: Islamic Dilemmas, 1985:110–117

10 Smith, Jane I.: Women in Contemporary Muslim Societies, 1980:116, 117

pattern follows exactly the same rules as apply to official dinner conversation in the West. A hostess would be ill-advised to speak out in the presence of a guest of honour, she would be very unwise to inform this guest about circumstances her husband would never wish to be disclosed. The number of females allowed to mix freely with men in Muslim countries remains limited to an extremely small group from westernised upper-class families who have been completely alienated from the culture of their own country.[11]

Thus the impression of Arab behaviour widely gained in Western circles as a consequence of closer contact with these latter families or representatives thereof may have led to total misconceptions. Whatever practical changes technological development may have brought about in daily life, it has certainly not lessened Islamic tradition. A number of popular books published by authors claiming to have insight and postulating to be reliable sources have rendered the Arab world most questionable services; they have rather contributed towards widening the gap in mutual understanding, very often distorting situations by omitting complementary explications, and biassing the readers by satisfying their expectations of the extraordinary or downright incredible.

1.5 Position of researcher

And the conscientious, ambitiously objective researcher? Mention must be made in this context of the phenomenon of an innate predisposition which infallibly influences the participating observer. One's mind is bound to think in line with the mental process one has been trained to follow, to automatically regard (and judge) a situation by this very system and not as an idiosyncratical feature of the person or circumstance observed. The concept one is accustomed to, which in German is so aptly referred to as "vertraute Begrifflichkeit", is too stubborn a travelling companion to permit any objective approach in a first encounter. The scrutinising mind of a person educated in the West, the trained, conclusion-oriented brain, avid to pigeonhole an experience and liken it to a familiar pattern, will be ready for insight into the unfamiliar only upon having parted with the inherent concept and having crossed the invisible border between two cultures, so that it will be conditioned to perceiving other structures, systems and actualities for what they are.

In this particular context it should perhaps be pointed out that what Western feminists consider a worthwhile target to obtain in the future development of

---

11 Kielstra, Niko: in Gellner, E.: Islamic Dilemmas, 1985:17

women might not necessarily correspond to the image the free Arab woman would wish to choose for herself.[12]

1.6 The Arab female researcher

The Arab female researcher will, on the one hand, have the advantage of familiarity with the cultural background – but will, on the other hand, be identified with her own (social) class when approaching informants. She will be expected to know many of the things a foreigner would be permitted to ask. She will also be expected to keep family secrets, not to divulge information revealed to her on the grounds of familiarity.[13] She may sometimes not collect a piece of information necessary for Western understanding of a situation – she would have to be genuinely familiar with the differences in the other culture in order to be aware which explanation is needed for the other side.

1.7 The Western female researcher

The Western female researcher is bound to meet with more difficulties in finding access. She will have to consider the time factor involved in establishing a relationship. Her participating observation may demand extreme adaptation. She will easily be at a loss to determine whether something is individually stated or a typical feature. She will have to be equipped with a fair amount of background knowledge or practical experience before being able to distinguish between conceivable alternatives and improbable deviations. But she has the advantage of being in a position to pose even what may be awkward questions, and of taking nothing for granted.

When carrying out research in an Arab country, both Arab and Western females share one problem though. An unmarried female is not considered legally valid, is pitied as an unfulfilled human being. No married (= knowledgeable) woman will be ready to confide in her. According to Islamic thinking and tradition only the consumption of marriage bestows womanhood.[14] And a woman who has not given birth to at least one child is considered a poor creature not in the grace of Allah, an ignorant and, at the same time, not someone eligible for a serious, matter-of-fact

---

12 Tucker, Judith E.: Arab Women, 1993:vii

13 Altorki, Soraya: At Home in the Field, in "Women in the Arab World", 1988:49 bis

14 Smith, Jane I.: Women in Contemporary Muslim Societies, 1980:12

conversation on mores and tradition. No matter how brilliant an academic career may have been accomplished by the aspirant, without these preconditions she will not be admitted as a "full woman".

In this context one could – as a further explanation for Western readers – refer to Goethe's "Iphigenie" to recall, as a conclusion of the above analysis, the unfortunately more difficult conditions women by nature have to cope with.

In the light of the foregoing it will be understood that two facts encouraged the author of this work to undertake the study: she had had ten years of close contact to the Arab World, five thereof with Yemen, and she is a married woman with children and grandchildren.

1.8 Choice of country

The reader will perhaps want an explanation with regard to the choice of the place of research and the reasons therefore:

Why was Yemen chosen for a study?

The Republic of Yemen before, and so far also after unification represents an excellent example of a genuine Arab country, geographically remote, looking back on a long tradition which has moulded her people and history. Yemen is a country which, although twice subjected to Turkish occupation, was never as a whole colonised by a Western power (the British protectorate covered the South Yemen only, and never extended to Sana'a) and, consequently, was never totally exposed to the direct influence of Western habits of living, ways of speaking, attitudes of behaviour. This is not the time to discuss the Imams and their ways of ruling, but it is an opportunity for alluding to the fact that the undiluted, pure spirit of Arab life inherent in the Yemeni population might be considered as a silver lining of the Imamat. This might also be an explanation why the so-called "Fundamentalist" movements[15] did not fall on fertile ground in the Yemen the way they did in other Islamic countries. The religious behaviour as encountered in Yemen reflects a

15 It might be interesting in this context to refer to a lecture given by Prof. Arne Ambros, Head of the Institute for Oriental Studies at Vienna University, in October 1993, referring to the very problematic aspect of the term "fundamentalist" as such – stubbornly adopted by the mass media while a much more appropriate term would be "reformist" in line with the underlying historic development and the original, essential doctrine involved.

natural, matter-of-course attitude, not heated by fanaticism but in no way negligent. And when the leader of the "Fundamentalist" movement in the Republic of Yemen wanted to address an audience, President Ali Abdullah Salah wisely agreed to a lecture at the military academy and attended the lecture himself.

Education has always been of particular importance to and for Yemenis. And although the last Imam was hostile to any influence from abroad, his educational programme was rather astounding. The fact that Yemen had 500 schools with an enrolment of 50,000 students by the 1940s spoke well for the Imam's educational system. Comparatively speaking, Yemen was far ahead of Saudi Arabia in the field of education in the 1920s and 1930s and still ahead in the early 1950s.[16]

Oil was discovered at such a late moment in Yemen that the country has been spared the culturally negative consequences of abundant amounts of petrodollars, has not had to rely on Western technology to exploit the country's resources, and has not imported Western styles together with Western know-how. And not only are the mud-walled dwellings, framed with graceful whitewashed lines like sugar icing on gingerbread, preserved intact, but the government actually issues few permits for new buildings over five storeys, and ensures that the ancient architectural style is respected, if not copied. The country has not yet been ruined by mass tourism, not because the number of visas is limited but because of the lacking infrastructure and the shortage of hotels.

In the Encyclopaedia Britannica[17] Yemen is referred to as:

"'Arabia Felix': ... the Greeks and Romans chose the name because of the area's pleasant climate and reputed riches in agricultural products and spices. The Emperor Augustus sent an expedition to Felix Arabia with disastrous results. Partly because of a native guide's treachery, the troops travelled by a circuitous way through waterless regions, so that they reached Southern Arabia weakened by disease, heat, and want of water..."

It is only fair to quote a myth in this context, the more so since it is the "explanation" furnished by Yemenis when asked why and how the country survived in the absence of modern technology, making a living in most astonishing and ingenious ways (and leading unwanted intruders astray):

---

16 Zabarah, Mohammad: Yemen – Traditionalism vs Modernity, 1988:17

17 Encyclopaedia Britannica, 1988:I:508;3a

"When God travelled the earth to distribute wealth and resources he completely omitted Yemen. When this was pointed out to him he considered the case for a long time and then resolved: 'Your gift will be a lucid mind and ingenuity and you will prosper by making use of this.'"

1.9 And why choose Sana'a?

When Altorki wrote her dissertation on "Women in Saudi-Arabia"[18] she defended her choice of elite families in a city by suggesting that an immense amount of field work was being done in rural areas, in highlands, in the countryside. A research project carried out in a city would therefore be a new challenge. Although this does not apply to Yemen at all, where the very opposite is true as Gingrich[19] clearly states in the introduction to his habilitation thesis, because cities are, in actual fact, the preferred objects of investigation, it would, in respect of this study, have been altogether impossible to cover the whole of Yemen. The choice of Sana'a provided a fascinating, feasible alternative, the more so in the expectation that a wider variety of differences might be encountered in a bustling city in relation to the relatively small area covered. But the choice is very much due also to the fact that this study is written by a city woman, much more familiar with crowded streets and multi-storeyed houses than with wide stretches of empty land and small settlements. In addition there was the thrill of investigating the differences between the women of an allegedly medieval metropolis in contrast to those of familiar European capitals. This on the basis of available literature on this subject:

As a start reference is made to an article by Roswitha G. Stiegner[20] on the position and status of women in ancient South Arabia, commenting i.a. on evidence found in respect of polyandry and matriarchate, on four different kinds of marriage – all in times long before Islam.

---

18 Altorki, Soraya: Women in Saudi-Arabia, Ideology and Behaviour among the Elite, 1986: Introduction

19 Gingrich, André: Der Agrarkalender der Munebbih, 1989:5–6

20 Stiegner, R.G.: Die Stellung der Frau in Altsüdarabien, in: Ausstellungskatalog des Museums für Völkerkunde, 1989:80

Fatima Mernissi[21] compiled a historic account of women in leading positions in Islam. In chapter VIII of her book "Sultanes oubliées" she refers to the "Queens of Sheba", depicting the attention and respect paid to two ruling queens at different times and the role and influence these ladies played and exerted.

Asmā' Yahyā al-Bāschā[22] contributed to the catalogue of the Yemen exhibition in Munich in 1987 by writing on women in Yemen in the old days and in modern times. She underlines the importance of women in political positions, deals with the legal status of women, family law, the new role of the Yemeni woman in the National Charta (**al-miṯāq al-watanī**), education and training, women's role in agriculture and women's unions.

Gabriele vom Bruck[23] furnished another contribution to this catalogue on the identity and change of women's life in Sana'a, emphasising two main aspects: the request for better incorporation into social and political affairs and, as a consequence, a reconsideration of Islamic values – the search for an alternative. She documents latest findings in the field of education and employment, changing attitudes in the choice of marriage partners, and also gradual changes in daily life and in the general outlook and in women's expectations.

More individual explanations and case studies were given by Carla Makhlouf[24] in her book on women and modernisation in North Yemen, and by Cynthia Myntti[25] in the 1972 GTZ publication on women and development in the then Yemen Arab Republic.

In her Middle Eastern ethnographic study "Women of ᶜAmran" Susan Dorsky[26] drew up an all-inclusive, richly documented and minutely illustrated report of her

---

21 Mernissi, Fatima: Sultanes oubliées, Femmes Chefs d'Etat en Islam, 1990

22 al-Bāschā, Asmā' Yahyā: Frauen im Jemen einst und jetzt, in: W. Daum, Ed. JEMEN, 1987:392-95

23 Bruck, Gabriele vom: Re-Defining Identity: Women in Sana'a, in: W. Daum, Ed. JEMEN, 1987:396–400

24 Makhlouf, Carla: Changing Veils, Women and Modernisation in North Yemen, London 1979

25 Myntti, Cynthia: Women and Development in Yemen Arab Republic, 1979

26 Dorsky, Susan: "Women of ᶜAmran", 1986

stay in this town and her endeavours to contact women and establish relationships, admitting the discouraging results at the start and recording the rewarding insight obtainable in the long run.

Detailed descriptions of female attire can be read in Martha Mundy's[27] article on Sana'ani dresses and outfit during the period 1920–1975, an account also rendering information on economic aspects and social considerations.

Gisela Frese-Weghöft[28], who spent long months in Yemen as a nutrition instructor, wrote about her very personal experiences in a book devoted to the invisible women (invisible = veiled). She succeeded in establishing close contacts to women from very different families and reports numerous informative details on their daily problems and ways of tackling them. She also candidly admits to not having managed to integrate and to having viewed her surroundings with affection but also a considerable amount of detachment.

Laurence Deonna[29], the Swiss reporter and journalist, having specialised in Arab and Middle East countries, produced a whole book to pass on information on her fantastic journey to, and experience gained with, the people of Yemen, where women apparently puzzled but also impressed her. Had she stayed longer she might perhaps have found certain aspects not so very hilarious.

There is an impressive group of women researchers and writers staying in Yemen at the present time. Their articles, books or reports will soon be published, to be added to the "Bibliography on Women in Yemen"[30], first edited in 1992.

---

27 Mundy, Martha: "San'ā' Dress 1920–1975" in R.B: Serjeant and R. Lewcock, 1983:529–540

28 Frese-Weghöft, Gisela: Ein Leben in der Unsichtbarkeit – Frauen im Jemen, 1986

29 Deonna, Laurence: Yémen, 1983

30 Buringa, Joke: Bibliography on Women in Yemen, ed. Martha Colburn, American Institute for Yemeni Studies, Westbury, New York 1992

1.10 A note on transliteration

The transcription of all Arabic terms used by the author of this study corresponds to that given in Hans Wehr: A Dictionary of Modern Written Arabic[31]. Where Arabic terms are translated into English, the definitions and explanations given are those found in this dictionary. This refers also to the footnotes and the spelling of names of persons or places or documents such as Mohammad, Mecca, Koran.

All Arabic terms and references appearing in texts quoted from other authors are given in the transcriptions used by the latter to the extent possible in standard text processing.

31 Wehr, Hans: A Dictionary of Modern Written Arabic, Fourth Edition, 1979

2. Introduction

2.1 Purpose of this study

While information on life in the Arab world had taken an unusually long passage to reach the West and information on women an even longer, the lacunae between general information and specific subjects are only gradually beginning to be filled. One of the most intriguing subjects of research on women is the status of women in Islam. When trying to establish a pattern of a woman's life and position under Islamic auspices, consideration should also be given to her position, chances, and titles in the context of inheritance. To do so the theoretical and practical circumstances must be analysed. How far does the law provide for individual subjects to inherit, how much is stated in respect of the female? To what extent is the law abided, followed, respected or disregarded? What are the practical circumstances influencing or having a bearing on law, or vice versa? How much is due to, or can be explained by, tradition, customary or tribal law?

In precise terms the formulation underlying the purpose of this study might read:

Do women inherit, and, if so, how?

To which must be added: how far can findings be documented, how much field work is necessary or desirable and what conclusions can be drawn, how many details need to be furnished to render a statement permissible?

2.2 The method adopted to meet this purpose

The method adopted in answering this complex question can be outlined as follows:

The study is an attempt in finding documentary evidence for the postulation that women do inherit. These documents are consulted, quoted and discussed with experts. Available literature is referred to for the purpose of confirmation or comparison. In order to test information obtained from documents, specific questionnaires were prepared, submitted to experts, and their replies are presented and discussed (Part One).

As the title of this study refers to "Law, Religion, and Reality", the reference to "Reality" is undertaken in the form of in-depth interviews with carefully selected informants. The notion "carefully selected" refers to the interviews actually presented. Informants were chosen from as wide a spectrum as at all possible and answers were incorporated or discarded with a view to avoiding repetition or the risk of misunderstanding – and very often also for the simple fact that cross-checking proved impossible or not sufficiently convincing (Part Two).

2.3 A presentation of Part One

All the interviews taken and recorded were prompted by considerations having cropped up during the elaboration of Part One.

Part One falls into two sections:

Section A – The legal system
comprises the sources of law and the judicial system. A short explanation of the legal education system is followed by an itemised summary of legal terminology. The historical background is then called upon and historical documents are scrutinised for relevant passages. Extracts are given from both historical documents and the legal gazettes in force, with special reference to the perpetuity of the provisions. Practical examples are taken from a handbook used by contemporary judges. The manifest importance of a special feature in Islamic inheritance, the rules of preclusion or prevention (**ḥujb**), is specially pointed out and illustrated by means of a table, as is the importance of the practical consequences of being a nearer or a farther relative, illustrated in a "generation model". The documentation is supplemented by questionnaires submitted to Imams and the Mufti.

Section B – Selected aspects of the legal system
deals with four special aspects of Islamic inheritance practices. The delicate issue of the female share is shown as seen by Muslim authors but also by the women actually concerned, the status of, and attitude towards, orphans and elopers is investigated, and special attention is given to two topics of particular importance in Islam, the **mahr** or bridal money which, as will be seen, plays a remarkable role in inheritance considerations, and **munāsik̲a** or postponement of the division of inheritance, a provision which might well be considered a clue to the assumption widely gained that women do not inherit, but should surely be referred to as compelling evidence to the contrary.

Before the presentation proper of Part One, some general remarks on Islamic Law are outlined, followed by a more specific general reference to inheritance laws.

2.4 Islamic law

The comprehensive system of personal and public behaviour which constitutes Islamic (religious) law is known as the Sharia (**šarī'a**), the revealed, or canonical law of Islam. Jurisprudence embarked on the turbulent course of reaching an understanding (**fiqh**) of this Sharia. In order to be able to do so, the principles or sources (**uṣūl**) from which such an understanding could be achieved had to be formulated. Legal theory stems from "the sources of understanding" (**uṣūl al-fiqh**).

The divine revelations vouchsafed by Allah to his chosen instrument, the prophet Muhammad, appear in two forms:

- in the text of the Koran;
- in the activities and decisions of the Prophet, known collectively as the Prophet's practice or **sunna**.

However, the two taken together in no way constitute a comprehensive code of law. The legal material they contain is a collection of piecemeal rulings on individual issues cropping up and dealt with on the spur of the moment. In the early days of Islam the existing customary law remained the accepted standard of conduct unless it was expressly superseded on a particular issue by a divine regulation. Where new circumstances posed new problems these were answered on the basis of what seemed the most proper solution in the personal opinion (**ra'y**) of the individual judge or jurist concerned.[32]

Understandably enough this could not satisfy Islamic scholars eager to establish an all-embracing legal basis in line with the fundamental doctrine of the omniscience and omnipotence of the Creator. They became known as "the supporters of hadith" (**ahl al-hadīṯ**), postulating that every rule of law must be derived either from the Koran or from the Prophet's practice as recorded in the reports known as **hadīṯ**, as opposed to "the supporters of ra'y" (**ahl al-ra'y**) who maintained that the free use of human reason was both legitimate and necessary.

---

32 The historical summary is an abridged version of Noel J. Couson: Conflicts and Tensions in Islamic Jurisprudence, 1969: Introduction and Chapter I

The compromise formula in this conflict was devised by the jurist Shafi'i and earned him the title of "father of Muslim jurisprudence".[33] While fully upholding the principle of divine revelation, he acknowledged the necessity for human reason to provide legal rules for situations not expressly or specifically directed by divine regulation. But this reasoning could not be in the form of ra'y, as this would imply the recognition of human reason along with, or parallel to, divine revelation. On the precondition that human reason must be entirely subject and subordinate to the principles established by divine revelation, the function of ra'y was to regulate new cases by applying to them the principles along which divine regulation had directed similar or parallel cases. This process is known as reasoning by analogy or **qiyas** which functions on the presumption that any process must find its starting point in an accepted manifestation of the divine will.

By way of a postscript, though, this legal theory recognised that in some cases strict analogical reasoning might entail injustice, and that in such cases more liberal reasoning should be authorised. For better distinction from the former "ra'y" a more sophisticated terminology encompassed this ultimate concession in terms of "**istihsan**" ("seeking the most equitable solution") or "**istislah**" ("seeking the best solution for the general interest"). This on the understanding that "equity" and "public interest" were divine purposes.

2.5 Inheritance laws in Islam

It is generally agreed among law experts in and outside the Islamic courts and repeatedly also referred to in Western texts that there is no topic better equipped to illustrate the interaction of the two elements of divine revelation and human reason than an inheritance problem. There is no issue in Islamic law of more pronouncedly individual characteristics than that of succession.[34] The meticulous precision with which the priorities of the different legal heirs are determined, and the quantum of their entitlement defined, is regarded as the zenith of juristic achievement and the showpiece of the whole legal system.[35] Reiterating the essential discrepancies in the

---

33 Incidentally, it was Shafi'i who coined the phrase: **"wa lā budda min Sana'a wa in tāli as-safar"** (Going to Sana'a is a must, no matter how long the journey may take) (personal communication by reference desk clerk at Sana'a University Library)

34 Schacht, Josef: An Introduction to Islamic Law, 1989:169–174

35 Bergsträsser's Grundzüge des Islamischen Rechts, bearbeitet und herausgegeben von Joseph Schacht, 1935:90-96

very concept of "law" and "legal", let it be emphasised yet again that "legal heirs" are such as a function of divine will, beyond the sphere of influence of the person they inherit from (or with some fairly small discretionary variants, although this would imply leaving the path of obedience to Allah's will, as will be amply discussed in parts I and II). According to a famous dictum of the Prophet, the laws of inheritance constitute "half the sum of all useful human knowledge"[36]. Also referred to as a labyrinth of legal complexity they are considered to represent the most typical expression of the spirit of Islamic legal thought.[37]

The laws of inheritance, furthermore, form a vital and integral part of the family law of Islam and might, in a sense, be said to constitute its focal point. The system of priorities and the quantitative value set on the entitlement of each relative derives from the position which that relative occupies in the scheme of family ties and responsibilities: rights of inheritance are the consideration for the services rendered to the deceased while he was alive (while not vesting the deceased with the power to acknowledge the type and extent of consideration paid to him by compensating the heirs therefor). The system mirrors the Islamic concept of social values and the structure of the family group, making it a fascinating, haunting and infinitely delicate subject for anthropological research.

What with the multitude of findings and opinions obtained, presented and discussed in the wake of a desired approximation between Occidental and Oriental patterns of society, any statement launched can be made on the comfortable cushion of quotable evidence. The aspiration of objectivity as the absolute goal of an impartial investigation will, on the other hand, sometimes cause uneasiness. Where open-minded curiosity is curbed to forestall the danger of personal involvement, this might curtail access to less obvious discoveries. Where data collected are labelled and pigeon-holed according to theoretical principles in the process of collection, they are likely to furnish valuable evidence for the validity of a theorem, but may not lead any further, while the danger of following a false line of investigation can be substantially minimised by assiduous cross-checking.

---

36 Delcambre, Anne Marie: Mohamet, La parole d'Allah, 1987:147

see also: Al-Shabassy, Eva und Omar, und Walters, Armin: "Allahs Gesandter hat gesagt ...", 1984:170

37 Hartmann, Richard: Die Religion des Islam, 1944:88–91

In this context the state of the art in this field is described in the respective literature[38] on

a) "the law of unrewarded effort" and

b) "the law of missing effect":

ad a) One of the results of research on commitment (to one's work) is the postulation that on the basis of the theory of cognitive dissonance[39] the individual adheres to a decision once adopted in respect of a theoretical assumption even in the event of non-confirmation by empirical research, but primarily makes increased efforts within the established concept, looking for further variables which might confirm the assumption instead of starting a line of thought outside the theory, or even revoking it.

ad b) It can be assumed that the selective perception of the researcher is of importance for the very structure of a concept although this is implicitly and also explicitly excluded from concepts as "not scientific" and "not objective" or is not even discussed. This can be understood to mean that the researcher claims a different behaviour for him-/herself – i.e. the rational-economic conception of objective behaviour – than the behaviour he/she imputes to his/her "objects of investigation", which is a subjectively evaluating behaviour guided by individual interests.[40]

2.6 Theory and practice

The above is stated as an opening for the assertion that "the truth", or, in less ambitious and more realistic terms, "an explanation" may perhaps not be found by digging for established findings in favour of an apparently convincing theory but by first examining all available material with a fair amount of hesitation or even suspicion, giving due consideration to the individual aspect of any contribution

---

38 Pfeffer, J.: Four Laws of Organ. Research, 1981:413, in: Strehl, Franz: Entscheidungsprozesse und ihre organisatorische Gestaltung als Grundlage von Reformprojekten, 1989:24

39 see also: Festinger, L.: Theory of Cognitive Dissonance, 1957

40 Pfeffer, J.: Four Laws of Organ. Research, 1981:414

offered, and by subsequently or simultaneously setting out to explore intellectually unfamiliar territory, equipped with an uncensorious mind.

If inheritance, laws of inheritance and actual practice are such complicated subjects where men, or "the male representatives of the species", are concerned, what a thorny path will be encountered by someone curious to explore the position of a woman in this maze? And this in a context and at a time when the very word "woman", the connotation of "female", has not ceased to be a bone of contention even in "advanced societies"?[41]

2.7 Women's rights in the context of "women in Islam"

Too much and too often the subject of "women in Islam" has been exploited by militant feminists, by followers of fashion in the context of women's liberation movements.[42] Many of the claims voiced at technical seminars and international conferences appear to be formulated with a disconcerting amount of disregard for, or unfamiliarity with, the actual situation in the field and the ideological concept of the women concerned.[43] A perusal of the respective resolutions, unanimously adopted and fully meeting the directives and regulations of international law, which have as yet to bridge the gap between wishful thinking and execution, makes the heart sink.[44] So do the many statements trying to explain the reasons for the unsatisfactory conditions so many women are exposed to by referring to women's ignorance of their rights and true position in society.[45] The legal rights of women as viewed by feminist researchers who are keen on pointing out the importance of adapting the law, and equalising rights, are hardly ever viewed in the context of the

41 Malti Douglas, Fedwa: Woman's Body, Woman's Word, 1992: Chapter III

42 Hjärpe, Jan: Islamic Fundamentalism and Women, 1983:12

43 Ahmed, Leila: Women and Gender in Islam, 1993:171 bis

44 Nicolaisen, Ida: Women in Islamic Societies, 1983:3

see also: Coulson, Noel & Hinchcliffe, Doreen: Women and Law Reform in Contemporary Islam, 1970:37–51

45 Many passages in the contributions on the subject of "Women in Islamic Societies" in "Studies on Asian Topics", 1983, testify to these attitudes.

economic reality nor that of the practical impact of a law.[46] In countries ravaged by famine, drought and natural catastrophes, economic disaster or political unrest, the issues at stake for the women are not rights and positions, and they cannot be expected to offer appreciation and gratitude for the efforts made in their name. Nor can they be expected to observe the instructions for achieving better positions. Their right to personal freedom and self-realisation is as much jeopardised as is their health and sheer survival, and they share this position on pitifully equal terms with men.

A closer look at the personal curricula vitae of "emancipated" women in Western societies, and in particular those of the indefatigable amazons for personal freedom and self-realisation, might suggest that their achievements be re-evaluated as to their suitability as models for imitation.

2.8 Economic background and social patterns

A much more positive approach towards the interpretation of the social pattern in which specific legal conditions are enshrined, would be a consideration of kinship models and forms of economic distribution, manifested in line with economic viability. This subject will be referred to in more detail in Part Two. The eternal dispute whether economic circumstances give rise to certain cultural behaviours, customs and habits, or whether the cultural background forms the basis for economic situations, stipulations and aspirations, in short the diverging opinions of Harris[47] and Sahlins[48], might be used as an example when attempting to explain

---

46 A suitable example in this context might be the tale of a woman encountered by coincidence as a next-door neighbour of a chosen informant. The woman had been one of the numerous daughters of a poor mountain farmer and had been married to a penniless qat-picker whom she dearly loved. She used to stay up all night to wait for her husband to return with his harvest, to be ready with a hot meal for him. The husband was very ambitious though. He left Yemen for Ethiopia and became a rich merchant. He married a second wife and ordered his first wife to return to Yemen where he set her up in style in a splendid house with servants and generous monthly payments. The first wife has ever since been in despair, looked after by her neighbours who pestered the researcher to tell them which legal provision would have helped her. They literally implored the interviewer to "help in creating laws against husbands becoming millionaires and no longer depending on the labour resources of women ...!"

47 Harris, Marvin: Good to Think or Good to Eat, 1985:13–18

48 Sahlins, Marshall: Culture and Practical Reason, 1976: Chapter 2

Islamic situations, too. Let it be expressly stated in this context that any such explanation will have to include pre-Islam patterns as pre-bases for any further considerations. But then Islam developed against the background of the prevailing conditions at the time when Muhammad received his revelations, and it would seem appropriate to assume that, for an understanding of why Islamic thinking was well received, it can be opined that the new religion fitted into the social pattern of those asked to become worshippers.[49]

2.9 Pre-Islamic doctrines

As we can read in "**al-mirāt̲ fi-š-šarī'a al-islamīya**"[50]:

"The new religion was based on a concept which agreed with the understanding of the people at that time, fitted into the ways of earning money and was in line with the continuation of their social life ..."

"And in respect to female inheritance in pre-Islamic times, evidence is contradictory and most sources state that there was no inheritance proper; some reports state that some of what was left by the deceased was for the woman, while other reports state that the woman inherited from her spouse and her next of kin. The custom to withhold inheritance from women was not with all the tribes a usual thing but only with some, and what is told concerns above all the tribes of the Hijaz."

"And in the time of the **Jahiliya**[51] it was also customary that only the son carried the father's name which entitled him alone to inherit what was left, until Islam came ... and improved the situation for the women." (Translated from Arabic)

Murtadā Mutahharī[52] offers one more "lucid" explanation of what was common practice before Islam:

---

49 Der Islam I, 1987:9-12

50 Daradka, Dr. Yasin Ahmad Ibrahim: 1983:38, 39, 85

51 **jāhilīya** = state of ignorance, pre-Islamic paganism

52 Mutahhari, Murtada: The Rights of Women in Islam, 1981:218

"The real cause of a woman's being deprived of inheritance was to prevent the transfer of family property to another family. According to the old idea, the role of the mother in the birth of a child was considered to be insignificant. Mothers were considered as mere containers in which the man's sperm developed, and out of which the child came into existence. For that reason they believed that the children of someone's son were the issue of a man, and thus they were part and parcel of his family. On the other hand, the children of his daughters were not his children, but the children of the husband of the daughter, and they belonged to the family of the husband of the daughter. Consequently, if a daughter inherited, and afterwards her children succeeded her, that would cause a situation where the wealth of one family would pass on to a different family."

It is understandable that many who still feel attracted by the philosophy of the insignificant role of women consider Islam as already extremely kind and generous towards the female component of the human race.

2.10 Women's inheritance – a fascinating topic?

Is female inheritance, consequently, an issue for research or a topic for philosophical discussions?

A topic related to women's inheritance in Islam will strike the eye and attention of jurists, anthropologists, sociologists, but likewise of economists and politicians, invariably, however, prompting criticism, incredulous surprise, derisive anticipation of downright failure. Quite apart from the fact that it proves an immensely difficult field of activity because of the innate controversy between the sexes, any attempt to offer the minutest contribution is destined to run the gauntlet of being exposed to evaluation and judgment on the basis of a by now dangerously popular image of the Muslim woman. Why should one bother to investigate the right of inheritance of a woman who by the very fact of her being a woman has no rights at all?

For a practical illustration of the encouragement the proposed topic received among representatives of the male sex approached in Sana'a, the following personal communication is presented:

In the office of the Head of the Economic Faculty[53] at Sana'a University where the idea of this study was first discussed, the faculty head, a very sociable scholar, produced a puzzled, amused smile. Sitting next to him were a lawyer and a young relative. The lawyer got to his feet to underline the importance of the matter and solemnly pronounced: "Women should inherit nothing, and if something is given to them they should let men look after it. They fare much better doing so. It is men who provide everything." To which the economist replied that surely the legal aspect of the subject should be referred to a judge. The young relative shifted his eyes towards the exit door. When the interview was over he was discovered in the corner of the staircase, voicing the following prophecy: "The key to female inheritance is not enshrined in studies and jurists' minds but in your understanding of womanhood in Islam."

In contrast to the above the project met with the full approval of Yemeni women. The reaction of those cautiously approached varied between expressions of outspoken relief that all of a sudden a Western researcher was not interested in collecting delicate details on virginity, sexual intercourse and polygamy, and a sympathetic smile that was later on to be interpreted in full as an indicator of how few facts can be traced showing practical adherence to the complex legal stipulations, and how differently inheritance as managed in real life presents itself. Promises of assistance were offered spontaneously and repeatedly, on several occasions with a reference to two apparently generally quoted proverbs:[54]

"**man jadda wajada**" (He who seeks diligently shall find),
and
"**iḏā aradt al-ᶜamal mutaqinan fa-anjuṯuhu binafsak**" (If you want a thing well done, do it yourself).

While men in general opined that no one not a good Muslim would be able to grasp how inheritance is administered, women went out of their way to find practical examples for, and contradiction to, the theories disclosed to them from the books and authorities consulted. Without their active participation and indefatigable support and kindness the unexpectedly cumbersome trail might have led to sheer

53 Dr. Abdul Aziz Al-Saqqaf, who is also the editor of "Yemen Times", not only smiled amusedly but also contributed in many practical ways and established most valuable contacts, for which many thanks are due to him.

54 The Adornment of Speech: A Dictionary of English and Arabic Proverbs, 1987:340 & 368.

despair. The respective passages in the Koran were discussed with the interviewer, were in most cases common knowledge learnt by heart in early childhood, and could be quoted by the majority of Yemeni women offhand. May it be permitted to point out that a distinct difference between Western women and Muslim women can be seen in the fact that the number of Western women versed with legal stipulations in respect of inheritance is somewhat restricted to those having received a legal education or otherwise studied the matter, while Muslim women, even when illiterate, by knowing the Koran know the rules of inheritance.

It is with the highest respect for the religious and philosophical importance and meaning of Islam that the following study is presented.

3. Part One

3.1 Section A – The legal system

Following the general outline on Islamic law in the Introduction, a summary of specific conditions as prevailing in the Yemen and/or as seen and interpreted by Yemeni **ʿulamāʾ**[55] or lawyers is given:

Since law in Islam is a part of religion, Yemeni law is a strictly religious law of a Muslim country, governed and represented by the religion as followed in the country. For a foreigner to become a Yemeni citizen it would be necessary to be a Muslim.[56]

The two religious schools prevailing in Yemen are the **zaidīya**[57] (zaidi) and the **šāfiʿī**[58] (shafi'i). No statistics are available as to the percentages; neither of the respective imams is ready to so much as hint at an approximate figure, and this not even for Sana'a. Families are either zaidi or shafi'i, but appear to accept the religious line of others as a natural variation, without any negative comment or even the smallest trace of disapproval or contempt. The fact that most **sāda** in Sana'a can be assumed to be zaidi[59] can be taken as one established feature, but does not permit any conclusion as to further actual distribution.

---

55 pl. of **ʿalīm** = the learned, the knowing

56 Law No. 2/1975 on citizenship, available in Sana'a also in English and German

57 The Zaidīya or Zaidi madhab (school of religious law) takes its name from Zaid b. ʿAli al-Husain, killed in Kufa in 740 in an insurrection against the Ummayads. His followers, originally supporting Zaid in opposition to Sunni rulers alongside the Shi'i movements of the time, developed a doctrine of their own and distinctive practices. See Gabriele vom Bruck: Descent and Religious Knowledge: Houses of Learning in Modern San'a, Thesis, 1991:97–101

58 One of the four Sunni schools, named after Al-Shafi'i, the "Father of Muslim Jurisprudence". The other three are the Hanafi, the Hanbali and the Maliki schools of thought.

59 The sāda consider themselves and are seen as descendants of the Prophet. Genealogies are drawn up, sometimes in tree-like fashion, and decorate the reception rooms of their houses. See: Gabriele vom Bruck, 1991:210

When, upon the creation of the Republic (1962), a special commission[60], set up for the purpose of drafting a modern legislation for the Yemen Republic, convened, the directives had explicitly been not to adhere to any one established school but to combine all those elements matching the need, on condition that no law would depart from either the Koran or the Sharia. A nation-wide codification was requested in order to put an end to regional versions. Representatives from all factions concerned were included. Laws were duly promulgated but to this day remain subject to constant revision, so as to be open for changes if the need arises.

But what were the elements the new constitutional legislation could be based on?

3.1.1 The sources of law

The sources of law are expressly mentioned in Law No. 10 of the 1979 Civil Law[61] (subsequently amended in other respects).

Article 1:

I. Law (legislation)
II. Principles of Sharia
III. Custom (not contradictory to Sharia) and
IV. Principles of justice (in agreement with Sharia)

ad I:

In pre-Islamic Arabia customary law was a living principle. The prophet Mohammad built upon the foundations of the tribal society, but replaced the old concept with that of the community of believers.[62]

In the world of Islam Muslim law is a body of authoritative legal norms elaborated in legal literature. It regulates many aspects of human experience, but it is mainly concerned with the authority of man over himself and his property, freedom of man and

---

60 Al Hubaishi, Husain: Legal System and Basic Law in Yemen, 1988:29

61 **mujallad qawānīn šarʿaīʼa** (Library of Sana'a University)

62 Al Hubaishi, 1988:51

the restrictions this entails, respect for promises, contracts and treaties signed, and other principles of natural law which are in agreement with the Islamic theory of law.[63]

In "Legal System and Basic Law in Yemen" Al Hubaishi states:
"According to the classical theory of Islamic law, the sources of law are as follows:

1 The Koran: the Muslim Holy Book, which is unalterable; it is the very word of Allah.

2 Hadith and Sunna: Hadith consists of the sayings of the Prophet, and Sunna means anything that could be proven to have been the practice of the Prophet and his oldest disciples.

Koran, Hadith and Sunna are the essential sources of Islamic law. The subordinate sources of law are[64]:

(a) Ijmaa[65]: that is the infallible consensus of the followers, for the Prophet said: 'My followers will never agree in error.'

(b) Qiyas[66]: that is the process of deducting by analogy according to the rules of logic. It is a source which, along with Ijtihad, does not depend on infallible divine inspiration, but rests on the judgment of men.

(c) Ijtihad[67]: that is personal reasoning, is based upon the 'jurist's' legal conscience, refined and disciplined by the intense and profound contemplation

---

63 Amin, S.H.: The Legal System of North Yemen, 1985:404

Amin is offered as a modern source of information on legal aspects in Yemen and therefore quoted here. However, special attention is drawn to an article in "Orient", the German Journal for Politics and Economics of the Middle East, in which Gingrich deplores the cursory approach and poor research the findings are based upon (ORIENT, 30. Jahrgang Nr. 2, June 1989:290).

64 For definitions of the four following terms see also: Encyclopedia of Islam

65 **ijmā'** = consensus of the authorities in a legal question

66 **qiyās** = comparison, analogy, deduction by analogy

67 **ijtihād** = independent judgment in a legal or theoretical question, based on the interpretation and application of the four **uṣūl** as opposed to **taqlīd**; individual judgment

of the law as entity. Incidentally, it is said that Ijtihad was first mentioned when the Prophet sent Muad bin Gabal to Yemen as ruler.

(d) Al Masaleh[68]: that is the general good or welfare, whenever an argument is general and ineffective. This is always the decisive argument, the principle being that the general prevails over the individual interest. This source was devised when the Muslim world expanded and legal problems differed from one region to another, so that the rulers had to exercise their minds."[69]

ad II:

Section 4 of the Constitution stipulates that "The Islamic Sharia is the source of all laws". Furthermore, Section 153 states that in the event of lacuna or if there is no provision in the Constitution or in the State Laws, and if there is no judicial precedent, the Courts shall pass their judgment in accordance with the general principles of the Sharia. By "general principles" is meant that no specific school of jurists must be followed exclusively. The reliance on the Sharia is a general commitment by many Muslim states as expressed in their constitutions in different phrases and terms.[70]

Although no specific school of jurists must be followed, legislation in Yemen is dominated by the schools of thought of the two main religious sects:

One is the Zaidi school, which is a bridge between the Sunni (the four orthodox schools) and the Shi'ite beliefs.[71]

The Shi'ites, in general, do not believe in Ijmaa or Qiyas, because to them their Imam is divinely inspired: yet the Shi'ites uphold the important source of Ijtihad; they have never believed that the gate to personal reasoning is closed.

---

68 maşlaḥa, pl. maşāliḥ = that which is beneficial, helpful or promoting

69 Al Hubaishi, 1988:52

70 ibid:53

71 As said and explained by Prof. Anderson in his lectures on Islamic Law (personal communication by former students)

The other largely prevalent school of thought in Yemen is one of the four orthodox schools, i.e. the Shafi'i.

The two schools generally differ only in certain questions of detail.[72]

In the context of female inheritance the following considerations present themselves:

- According to Sunni opinion, which could be referred to as being represented in Yemen by the Shafi'i school of thought, any surplus after distribution of obligatory shares should go to the mortmain (**bait al-māl**).

- Al-Qasim[73] is reported to have decided against the Shi'ite rule of thought (also) in inheritance matters. He did not grant the holders of obligatory shares a claim to further distribution of any surplus, and fully excluded the **ḏawū-l-arhām** (relatives through a female = through the womb).[74]

- According to Zaidi opinion, this surplus is also to be distributed to the holders of obligatory shares, and the **ᶜaṣabāt** and the **ḏawū-l-arhām** are entitled to inherit.

- For the Shi'ites this question was also important as regarded the claim to inheritance of Ali's followers as descendants of the Prophet's daughter, Fatima. But al-Qasim repudiated any such claim on the grounds of the fact that the Prophet had distributed everything he possessed to the community before he died.[75]

---

72 Al Hubaishi, 1988:54

73 al-qāsim = Imam al-Qāsim b. Ibrāhīm, born 169 a.h., the founder of the zaidi school of law, honoured for establishing religious provisions that united the representatives of the zaidi sect in Yemen. He was the son of Ibrāhīm b. Ismā'īl Tabāṭabā, who participated in the revolt of al-Husain b. ᶜAli b. al-Hasan.

For a biography see Wilferd Madelung, 1985:86 bis

74 Madelung, Wilferd: Der Imam al-Qasim b. Ibrahim und die Glaubenslehre der Zaiditen, 1979:134

75 ibid:135

In his contribution in respect of "Shi'i Attitudes Towards Women as Reflected in Fiqh", Madelung refers to the "abolition of the privileged position which the Sunni law of inheritance accords to agnates in favour of a roughly equal treatment of relatives related through male and female links."[76] But this does not really apply to female inheritance in the Yemen context, as the Mufti, two imams of mosques and a lawyer pointed out in personal interviews and/or in their written replies to questions submitted in writing (copies are attached and a translation is given), and these Yemeni experts maintain that Zaidi law is not Shi'i.

One might also cite an explanation frequently offered by ordinary Yemenis that the **zaidīya** is somehow in between the **imamīya** (the "orthodox" Shi'i) and the main-stream Sunni line of thought. Or, in another imagery: **al-manzila bayn al-manzilatayn** (a position between two positions)[77].

ad III:

Custom, or **ᶜurf**, may be considered one of the most delicate subjects in legal thinking. It is today generally agreed that **ᶜurf** is admissible as long as it does not contradict Sharia. While Chelhod[78] points out that "le fossé est en effet grand entre le Yémen de la Constitution, qui n'admet comme loi que celle de l'Islam, et celui de l'éthnologue qui y découvre une mosaique de groupes très éloignés les uns des autres et où prédomine bien souvent la coutume"[79], discussions with **quḍā'**[80] create the impression that if disputes can be settled according to custom, habit and general

---

76 Madelung, Wilferd: Shi'i Attitudes Towards Women as Reflected in Fiqh, 1979:71

77 A theological term originally used by the later **muᶜtazila** for designating the salvation status of the mortal sinner. The equivalent translation was: "Salvation between paradise and hell".
As Dr. Eisenstein from the Institute for Oriental Studies at Vienna University kindly explained it is now understood to refer to a point of view being taken between two points of view as compared to an uncritical adoption of either.

For more details see Encyclopaedia of Islam or Wilferd Madelung, 1985:10 bis

78 Chelhod, Joseph: La Société Yéménite et le Droit, 1975:67

79 The gap is indeed considerable between the Yemen (as encountered) of the Constitution, only allowing the law of Islam, and that of the social anthropologists, discovering a mosaic of groups greatly differing from each other and often governed by custom.

80 pl.of qāḍi = judge

opinion, no further legal proceeding is required. Gingrich offers a transparently clear definition of **ᶜurf** which is here given to the extent applicable in the context of this study (translated from German): "The root of **ᶜurf** is "to know, to be aware", and this refers to those parts of customary law that are generally known. ᶜurf is common knowledge of a society, with which every adult member (of the tribe) vested with legal capacity is familiar and which is passed on exclusively by word of mouth to every further generation ... This refers i.a. to questions of property and inheritance law, divorce, assistance obligations and the responsibility therefor, but also to the basic question of who is vested with legal capacity and who is not, and who is the legal authority in a household or among in-laws ... **ᶜUrf** thus provides implicit rules of behaviour in interaction with the principles of the kinship pattern, and regulations for the settlement of every-day, recurrent disputes. Only where such disputes cannot be settled amicably by those concerned or in consultation with in-laws, is an intermediary approached."[81]

ad IV:

The principles of justice are once again required to conform to the Sharia. Article (1) of Part 1 in the 1979 Civil Law stipulates that "If the judge finds no provision in this law to apply he shall refer to the principles of Islamic Sharia, customs, or principles of justice. The judge is not allowed to construct or pronounce legal rules but only to apply them. If there is no such rule, the judge may resort to general principles of law deduced by way of jurisprudence or comparative law, provided the justice sought after is sanctioned by the principles of Sharia".[82]

81 Gingrich, André: Der Agrarkalender der Munebbih, 1989:118

82 Al Hubaishi, 1988:73

3.1.2 The judicial system

"A salient characteristic of the Yemeni judicial system is its cleavage into almost parallel systems of traditional and modern courts ... Until recently the clerical hierarchy possessed a near monopoly of legal literacy and litigation and the language which it employed in writing is not identical with any spoken idiom. The great legal fiasco continued merrily until late in the sixties."[83]

To remedy this situation and meet the requirements of a modern state, not only were the laws codified, the whole system was constitutionalised (Article 144 of the Permanent Constitution of 1970).

3.1.2.1 Legal education

For a very long time judges were exclusively educated at the mosque. To become a qadi it was customary to stay for a number of years as an apprentice with the Imam of a mosque or to go to a religious or semi-religious school (madrasa) and learn everything that was considered necessary for the profession. Only in 1970, in the wake of Yemen's opening towards Western education, was the faculty of law installed at Sana'a University. While all established jurists of the traditional pattern are permitted to retain their positions, newcomers are now requested to graduate at the University and to subsequently undergo further training at a "Higher Institute". To be admitted as a lawyer, the graduate must serve under a registered lawyer for a certain period before being granted the right to go to the Bar. Admission to higher courts requires longer periods of apprenticeship. Lawyers must register with a Committee of the Ministry of Justice and the Legal Advisors' Office to obtain official permission to practise. Admission to various levels in the judiciary is governed by experience.[84]

3.1.2.2 Legal terminology

For better understanding of the connotations and underlying configurations of passing on or exchanging titles and property in Islam today, let us look at the documented definitions of the respective terms as given by Arab lawyers.[85]

---

83 ibid: 139

84 Amin, S.H.: The Legal System in North Yemen, 1985:410

85 ur-Rahman, Tanzil: A Code of Muslim Personal Law, Vol. II, 1980:99 bis

Gift (**hiba**): The transfer of movable or immovable property with immediate effect and without counter-consideration by one person in favour of another, and the acceptance of the same by that other himself or by someone authorised on his behalf is called "gift", provided that the one making the gift of his independent free will totally renounce all his titles and rights in the property gifted away.

The basis of the principle of gift is the Prophet's saying "Exchange gifts among yourselves so that love may increase (**taḥādū' – taḥābū'**)".

"Gift" may also be referred to in Arabic as **ṣadaqa**, **nahlah** and **ᶜatiyah** (donation), but must not be confounded with **ᶜariyat** (transfer of a limited interest). **ᶜAriyat** refers to some limited interest in the benefits, produce, profit or usufruct of a property for a limited period. In other words, **hiba** is a transfer of ownership without counter-consideration and **ᶜariyat** is a temporary licence to enjoy the profits so long as the grantor pleases.

Waqf, pl. **awqāf** (endowment, dedication), is a transfer of the corpus of valuable property to the ownership of Allah with a declaration dedicating its usufruct perpetually for religious, charitable or pious purposes as recognised by the shari'a.

There are, in actual fact, two kinds of **waqf**:[86]

waqf khayri for religious purposes, and
waqf dhurri for the management of family property,

with the latter type playing an important role in women's economic positions and their access to property, and also management of property.

Shaykh Fadhlalla Haeri[87] defines **waqf** as: "pious endowment or foundation of certain incomes (commonly rents or land revenues) for the upkeep of a mosque, a hospital, etc. Sometimes the main purpose of such endowment was to provide entailed and unconfiscable income for one's descendants".

(As was commented in personal communications, the number of **awqāf** is declining in modern times, they are more or less running out. The creation of a **waqf** is

86 Meriwether, Margaret L.: in: Arab Woman, 1993:71

87 Haeri, Shaykh Fadhlalla: The Elements of Islam, 1993:160

considered "obsolete" or even "a nuisance", and is regarded as an act of "wilful encumbrance of practical proceedings.")

The estate (**tarika**) is that property which the deceased (ancestor) leaves behind him as his lawful property, and in respect to which there is no right of another particular person attached. A property which the deceased has usurped or stolen or acquired through dishonest means such as bribe may not be included in the estate.

Lawyers furthermore explicitly state that "if a stranger's right is attached with the estate, e.g. under mortgage, that property shall not be termed as estate of the deceased till the stranger's right does lapse or is paid up. And if property is submerged in debt it shall not devolve upon the heirs. If not submerged, it shall be divided among the heirs after payment of debts".

No uniform opinion can be discovered as regards the so-called "titles" or "rights" (**ḥuqūq**). Whether or not the right of residence or the right of usufruct can be registered as constituting part of an estate and hence be passed on to heirs, is very often considered negotiable only in as far as directly related to tangible estate, i.e. transfer of the actual property. It would appear understandable that the right of residence or usufruct would have to be renegotiated between the holder of such rights and the actual heirs of the respective property.

Existence of an estate

If the deceased left no estate and was in debt, this debt shall not be due and recoverable from the heirs in as much as the creditor's right is linked with the estate of the deceased and not with the person or the property of the heirs. In such a case, therefore, the presence or otherwise of heirs is immaterial. If an heir, in spite of there being no estate left by the deceased, pays up the debt due from the deceased, his action shall be ex-gratia, for which he shall be entitled to a reward in the next world.

Legal character of the estate

In the event of the deceased leaving property it is essential that the same be lawful and lawfully acquired. The unlawful and forbidden possession of pecuniary rights, therefore, cannot be considered to be open to inheritance under the law of shari'a, for instance wine stores or money won in horse racing or lottery or drawn from insurance or immoral films or obtained by fraud, usurpation or as bribe or **riba** (interest).[88]

However, in countries wherein such practices have received legal sanction the heirs shall be entitled to such properties and share them in accordance with the laws in force in those countries and not as dictated by shari'a.[89]

Below are listed relevant definitions as quoted in the respective Yemeni Law Gazette[90]:

al-arṯ:	the process of inheritance, when property and titles of the deceased are passed on
al-muwāriṯ:	the person who dies or is declared dead by a court
al-wāriṯ:	the one who inherits because of a kinship relation or through marriage
al-mawrūṯ:	the property and titles left by the deceased
as-sabab:	the cause without which there would be no entitlement
al-mānaᶜa:	preclusion to inheritance
al-farḍ:	the fixed share as laid down in the Sharia, which can only be increased by **radd** or decreased by **ᶜawal**
radd:	additional inheritance upon division of the remainder (if the total of all fixed shares amounts to less than the actual legacy) excluding the wives; if there is no **ᶜāsab**
ᶜawal:	reduction in inheritance if upon division of the total legacy according to fixed shares there is a deficit (the reduction is made in proportion to the fixed shares)

88 = usurious interest

89 ur-Rahman, Tanzil: 1980:402 bis

90 **al-qarār al-jumhūrīy bi-l-qānūn raqm** 20/1992: Chapter 6

ᶜāsab:	a person not entitled to a fixed share who gets the remainder; that same person may get everything if there are no receivers of fixed shares
ᶜāsab bi-nafsihi:	a male relative in the ascendant generation whose relationship with the deceased does not go through a female
ᶜāsab bi-g̅airihi:	a female who needs someone else to be entitled to share the right to inherit
ᶜāsab ma-g̅airihi:	a female not requiring someone else to be entitled to share the right to inherit
ḥujb:	exclusion (fully or partially) from shares in inheritance
d̲ū-ar-raḥm:	every relative not entitled to a fixed share and not an **ᶜāsab**
al-jadd aṣ-ṣaḥīḥ:	a person from the former generation, related to the deceased by males only (not through a woman)
al-jadda aṣ-ṣaḥīḥa:	a true grandmother is a woman whose husband (the grandfather) inherits in the line between her and the deceased
al-k̲untā' al-muškil:	the problematic sex (hermaphrodite) where it is not clear whether the person is male or female
al-mafqūd:	a missing or lost person where it is not proven whether someone is dead or alive
al-walad az-zanā:	illegal child, when the relationship with the deceased is not proven by a rightful marriage contract
al-walad al-laᶜān:	a child of the "curse the liar" type, i.e. a child from a dissolved marriage. The child is the divorced husband's child unless disavowed by the father
aṣl al-masāla:	the smallest fraction permitting of division

at-taṣīḥ:	all the shares and also the total must be calculated using the common denominator

3.1.2.3 Historical background of inheritance rules

On the assumption that all guidance provided by the Koran, that is to say all that is found in terms of "directives", was occasioned by one particular situation having cropped up, it will be asked what this situation might have been in terms of inheritance rules?

In his "Handbuch des Islamischen Gesetzes nach der Lehre der schafi'itischen Schule", Juynboll[91] records that in the year 3 after the Hidjra[92], after the Battle of Uhud, when amongst others ᶜAus b. Thābit had been killed, his widow is said to have approached the Prophet, bitterly complaining that two male blood relatives of her late husband intended to take all that was left for themselves; this would mean that she and her minor children would become entirely destitute. The Prophet took pity on the widow and her children. He received a revelation which gave rise to verse 8 in Surat an-Nisa' as a first advice. The prophet ordered that the inheritance of Aus b. Thabit was to be left untouched until further notice, until Allah had sent him further revelations. Only after revelations 12 to 15 had been passed on to him, did the Prophet proceed to decide on the further division of the inheritance. Juynboll concludes that although this story cannot be verified for its historical value it permits the reflection that the number of warriors killed at that time and leaving their survivors with multiple problems of inheritance might well have given rise to the Koranic revelations.

3.1.2.4 Historical documents

3.1.2.4.1 The Koran

For the sake of completeness and easier reference the respective passages of the Koran are quoted in the translation by Richard Bell[93], including the headings and explanatory footnotes where appropriate:

---

91 Juynboll, Th.W.: Handbuch des Islamischen Gesetzes, 1910:237–238

92 = the emigration of the prophet Mohammad from Mecca to Medina in 622 A.D.

93 Bell, Richard, B.D.,D.D.: The Qur'ān, 1960:68 bis

Surat an-Nisa' – Chapter of the Women

Inheritance of relatives

12. In regard to your children Allah charges you (as follows): The male receives the portion of two females; if they be women[94], more than two, then they receive two-thirds of what a man has left, but if there be only one, she receives a half; his parents receive, each of them, a sixth of what he has left, if he have children; but if he have no children and his parents heir him, then his mother receives a third; if, however, he have brothers, his mother receives a sixth – (this) after any bequests he may have made or debts (have been paid); whether your fathers or your sons are of most benefit to you[95], ye know not – an ordinance from Allah, verily Allah hath become knowing, wise.

13. A half of what your wives leave belongs to you if they have no children; if they have children, a fourth of what they leave belongs to you, after the bequests they have made or debts (have been paid);

14. To them belongs a fourth of what ye leave, if ye have no children; if ye have children, an eighth of what ye leave belongs to them, after any bequests ye may have made or debts (have been paid).

15. If a man – or a woman – whose property falls to be inherited have no direct heirs, but have a brother or a sister, each of the two receives a sixth; if there be more than that, they share in the third, after any bequests he may have made or debts (have been paid).

And also

175. (referred to as a later modification of 15)
They ask thee for a deliverance; say: "Allah giveth you a deliverance in regard to the person who leaves no direct heirs; if a man perishes and has no children but a sister, the half of what he leaves belongs to her; and he is her heir, if she have no children; if there be two (sisters), the two-thirds of what he leaves belongs to them; if there be brethren, male and female, a share

94 if there be no male children

95 or "most entitled to benefit you"

equal to the portion of two females belongs to the male; Allah makes clear to you lest you err; Allah everything does know."

16. Without prejudice one to the other; a charge from Allah; verily Allah is knowing, gracious.

17. These are the limits laid down by Allah; whoso obeys Allah and His messenger He will cause to enter Gardens through which the rivers flow, to abide therein – that is the great success.

18. But whoso opposes Allah and His messenger and transgresses the limits laid down by Him He will cause to enter a Fire to Abide therein, and for him is a punishment humiliating.

Treatment of orphans

2. Bestow upon the orphans their property; do not substitute the bad for the good, and do not consume their property in addition to your own – verily it has become a great crime.

3. If ye fear ye may not act with equity in regard to the orphans, marry such of the women as seem good to you, double or treble or fourfold – but if ye fear that ye may not be fair, then one (only) or what your right hands possess;[96] that is more likely to secure that ye be not partial[97] – and give the women their dowries as a gift; if, however, they of their own pleasure give some of it to you, enjoy it with satisfaction and good conscience.

4. But do not give to those of weak intellect the property which Allah has appointed you to manage, but feed them and clothe them and speak to them in reputable fashion.

5. Make trial of the orphans until they reach (the age of) marriage, then if ye perceive right management of them, hand over their property to them; do not consume it in extravagance or in anticipation.

---

96 i.e. slaves

97 or "be not over-burdened with children"

6. of their growing up; let him who is rich restrain himself (from touching it) and let him who is poor use it reputably;

7. then when ye hand over their property to them, call witnesses against them – Allah is sufficient reckoner.

8. To the men belongs a portion of what their parents and near relatives leave, and to the women belongs a portion of what their parents and near relatives leave, be it little or much; a (legally) assigned portion.

9. When the relatives, the orphans, and the poor are present at the division, provide for them out of it, and speak to them reputably.

10. Let those who if they (themselves) were to leave behind them a weak posterity would be afraid on their account, beware; let them act piously towards Allah, and pronounce a straight-forward decision.

11. Verily those who consume the property of orphans wrongfully, only consume fire in their own bellies, and will eventually roast in the Blaze.

Property of wives

23. O ye who have believed, it is not permissible for you to heir women against their will;[98] and do not tyrannise over them that ye may go off with part of what ye have given them, unless it be that they commit a manifest indecency; associate reputably with them; if ye dislike them, it is possible that ye may dislike a thing in which Allah hath set much good.

*3.1.2.4.2 Sharia (**šarīᶜa**) or codification of Islamic law*

The official book of reference for Islamic law in Yemen is the Commentary according to the Hanafitic School of Islamic Law. From the four-volume compendium of this **šarḥ al-azhār**[99] two extracts are quoted in translation. Since the respective texts are written in an Arabic of times gone by, the translation is given as literally as possible but with due interpretation of the annotations and explanations

---

98 Probably referring to putting pressure on a wife to compel her to bequeath her property to the husband.

99 **šarḥ al-azhār (al-imām al-murtafa')**, vol. 3/1341 und vol. 4/1342 a.h. editions.

without which some passages would be entirely incomprehensible, and footnotes are given, where explanations had to be provided by members[100] of the Faculty of Law at Sana'a University approached for that purpose.

The following passages are quoted also in view of the fact that numerous questions about inheritance rules are already answered by merely reading through the text.

Volume 3, page 381

Chapter on Division:

When mentioning the conditions for the division, be aware that there are seven of them, and five of these concern the correctness (and two are for the enforcement of the law if someone refuses to abide by the five).

First Condition:

What is necessary for a correct procedure is the presence of the owners/holders of the shares or their representatives, and always a representative of anyone absent or of a rebel[101] or of a minor standing up for them, or an authorisation of anyone present to stand up for them. But if these conditions are not followed then the absentee or the minor has the right to cancel the proceedings (refuse to accept the decision), except in the case of measurements or weighing procedures, where it is permitted that everyone takes his or her share, even if the others have not attended (were not represented) because the division is even (amounts of the same matter).

---

100 Muhammad Yahya Al-Makhadi
Numan Abdallah Ibrahim
Abdallah Muhammad Aqlan
(given in the transcription as indicated by the holders)

101 A rebel **(mutamarrid)** is a person excluded or disclaimed by the family for bad behaviour or because it is ashamed of him, or who is in jail, but nevertheless still entitled to inheritance. The example given was the following:

"A very irksome father had behaved so infuriatingly towards his son that the latter one day threw a huge stone at him, hitting him so hard that the father suffered severe injuries and cursed and disclaimed his son. He was no longer considered a member of the community and was sentenced to three years in prison. During this period the father died. The son was given his share as provided for in the Koran, and it was handed over to him when he left the prison." (personal communication)

Second Condition:

(Evaluation of different quality) For things that are different, such as those which have different prices, i.e. land, etc., so that it is not permitted to divide by dimension but by evaluation, and by making up for differences either in terms of amount or weight or dimension, whatever is applicable – but if the division is made without doing this, it is not correct.

Third Condition:

Everyone must get his or her share either personally or via the representative. But if the share of a minor or absentee is handed over to someone who spends it or neglects to look after it – it is not correct. And if a shareholder takes his share from measured things, this is permitted on condition that the other shareholders (also) get their shares (later).

Fourth Condition:

The division of common rooms must be such as to least affect the other shareholders, e.g. if a house is divided, that not one of them gets the corridor, or will not have a stream of running water[102], and the division must be repeated unless agreement is reached. And also if for instance land is divided and there is a well on it, access to the well must be divided too.

Fifth Condition:

Division must not deal with what is left behind by a man who has debts until all the creditors have been satisfied by a sale, since once a person has inherited he is not responsible for debts.

And there are two supplements to the Second Condition:

* and to facilitate division (make easy the difficult) a share should be calculated on a possible division basis (i.e. as a fraction). And a share must consist of land if land is distributed and must not be replaced by money, except if there is a road on a piece of property, or if the division concerns gowns or animals, in which case a replacement by other things is possible.

---

102 masīl al-mā' = toilet (considering the times when this text was written, this is an impressive indication of the standard of water supply in these houses).

And the second item of the Second Condition:

* a division must not be followed by another division, i.e. 1/2 – 1/3 – 1/6, but if you start by dividing into sixths a solution is possible, except when agreement is reached that shares will be completed by different types of matter – then the division is correct.

Volume 4, page 469

Section on Wills

A will is an authorisation from one adult to another to stand for him after death in certain matters, and the basis for this from the Koran is what Allah said: "It is an obligation for you that when death comes to one of you who leaves valuables that you pass them on." And in the Sunna the saying of the Prophet – Peace be upon him – is that it is not correct for a Muslim who has something to will to stay two nights without his will under his head, i.e. the meaning of this expression is that there is nothing more important and more correct than this and there is no disagreement on the priority of this.

3.1.2.4.3 ***kitāb al-ahkām fi-bayān al-ḥalāl wa al-ḥarām***
Book of religious rules in showing the permitted and the forbidden

In his commentary on religious rules, Imam Yahya bn al-Husain[103], founder of the Zaidi religious law, devotes 50 pages or 47 chapters on the religious rules in showing the permitted and the forbidden.

The introduction to **farā'iḍ**[104] law is a summary of the Koranic verses. Chapters 1 to 17 then deal individually with every single heir, with the chapter headings already detailing the following contents, such as Chapter 3 "on who of the women inherit and how many of them inherit" or Chapter 7 "on whom the mother prevents from inheriting and who precludes her from her one third".

Chapter 3 appears particularly suited for an understanding of the detailed manner of stipulating inheritance rules so that a literal translation is given:

---

103 Imam Yahya b. al-Husain: **kitab al-ahkām fi-bayān al-halāl wa-l-harām**, 1457 a.h. edition

104 **farīḍa,** pl. **farā'iḍ** = religious duty, ordinance of God, obligatory (shares)

"The women who are entitled to **farā'iḍ** are only seven, and these are mentioned in the Koran:

for the daughter 1/2
for daughters, if there be more than one, 2/3
for the mother 1/6
if there are children or sisters and brothers (of the deceased) the sister gets 1/2
and two or more sisters 2/3
and a sister from the mother only 1/6
and a wife 1/8, if there are children, and 1/4, if there are not

and (not in the Koran but according to Sunna)
those women who can inherit, are nine:
three of them inherit in all cases, and six are prevented in some cases,
and the three who inherit in all cases are
the daughter, the mother, and the wife,
and the six others are
the grandmother, the full sister, the sister from the father only and the daughter of the son, and the sister from the mother only, and a freed slave."

Chapter 17 deals with the inheritance of the so-called **kalāla**, a term no longer mentioned in more modern texts nor in current law books, but still used by **ʿulamā'**. A **kalāla**[105] is a person dying without children, nor parents nor a grandparent, in which case the brothers and sisters receive bigger shares, and no one prevents them or reduces their shares.

Chapter 18 renders instructions on "suspension" of inheritance (**munāsika̱**). It may occur that someone dies and the heirs do not divide the inheritance but wait until a further person dies, so that further heirs come in. (This chapter is of particular importance also in respect of females, and is, therefore, specially pointed out here. The right to suspend is very often employed to keep family property together – in many cases property in the hands of men, who also look after the women's shares. Women tend to agree to such procedures which leave them in better bargaining positions and will be of special interest for their children upon a mother's death.)

105 al-Maridi, Yahya Ahmed b.: **al-baḥr az-zājar**, vol. 6:324

Since **munāsika** renders the division of an inheritance even more complicated than an ordinary division already is, the mention of this feature is always followed by a practical example. Thus chapter 18 goes on to read (in translation):

"... a man dies and leaves a wife and two sons, but they do not divide before one of the sons dies; and then they first divide the first **tarika** into 16 shares, 2 for the wife = 1/8, and what remains is for the two sons = 14 shares, divided by 2 = 7 shares each. And when one of the two sons dies, leaving a mother and a brother, the second division reads:

1/3 for the mother,
2/3 (the rest) for the brother,

and his share is 7 from the first **tarika** but 7 cannot be divided by 3, so the division is done in threes, i.e.:

1 share for the mother and 2 shares for the brother,

but this does not correlate with the first division. In this case we multiply both denominators with each other:
3 x 16 = 48
and then divide 48 by the shares:

6/48 for the mother,
21/48 for the brother,

and from the 21/48 left by the dead brother:
the mother takes 7/48 and the brother 14/48,

so that the mother gets 13/48,
and the son 35/48.

The respective chapters on **ᶜawal** (19) and **radd** (20) are defined in shorter terms in the Yemeni legislation, as are the chapters on the **dawū al-arḥām** (29), who are among other specifications referred to as the "people not mentioned in the Koran nor the Sunna", and the chapter on the inheritance of the cursed child (31).

Quite exhaustive are chapters 22 and 25, the first on "inheritance of the drowned and the burnt and the destroyed and the lost and what happens to their shares", stating that in such cases attention must be paid towards establishing who drowned before whom etc. in order to determine the correct succession of heirs; and the latter on "a dead person leaving a pregnant woman, but the division having been done in a hurry before it became obvious what the pregnancy is".

Chapter 24 refers to "bisexual heirs" whose gender for the purpose of respective shares is stated to require an examination at court, when the person must stand against a wall and urinate against it. If he/she can do so, a full share is allotted, if not, only a half share.

Chapters 35 – 47 deal with all the items referred to before but in relation to slaves.

3.1.2.5 A handbook of inheritance as used in Sana'a

For practical examples, even if still on a theoretical basis, an Arab Handbook[106] was studied and excerpts are given:

*3.1.2.5.1 **ḥujb** table*

The following table of exclusion/prevention (**ḥujb**) is already provided in the introduction to the handbook and is referred to as a basic instrument for proper calculation:

Table of exclusion/prevention (**ḥujb**)

Group 1 (holders of obligatory shares)	
1	The grandfather is excluded by the father and the nearer grandfather prevents the farther
2	The grandmothers are excluded by the mother – see inheritance of the grandmothers
3	The son's daughter is excluded by sons or the son's son and two daughters above her unless there is a father's son's son or father's brother's son equal to her in grade or below her, if she did not get an obligatory share
4	The full sister is excluded by the father and the son and the son's son and a next following son and the sisters, if they have sons as they are relatives from the father's side (and pay attention to the vast possibilities)
5	The sister from the same father is excluded by the father and the son and the son's son or his son, and the full brother and the full sister if there is a full sister with daughters, and is excluded by two full sisters, unless there is a blessed brother inheriting the rest with her
6	The brothers from the same mother (only) are excluded by the lineage and by the inheriting children and farther children

106 Al-Ḥanbālī, Muhammad Sᶜaīd, **Uṣūl ᶜilm al-mawāriṯ**, 1985

And observed and respected in the determination of the number is the preceding line, degree of kinship and strength of bond, since a nearer grandfather excludes a farther one and the father's brother and his son, whether full or from the same father only, and the father excludes the grandfather's brother, even if he is a full one, and thus the grandfather's brother and his son exclude the greatgrandfather's brother, even if he is a full one.

Please note: Imam Abu Hanifa said the grandfathers have the effect of the fathers and exclude the brothers completely.

Group 2 (ᶜaṣabāt)		
1 The son's son	is excluded	by the son as is every farther relative by a nearer one
2 The full brother	is excluded by 3 categories:	father, son, grandson and his children
3 The brother from the same father	is excluded by 5 categories:	the above 3 plus full brother or full sister if she is ᶜāṣaba with the daughters
4 The full brother's son	is excluded by 7 categories:	grandfather, father, son, grandson and his children full brother brother from the same father full sister or sister from the same father if she is ᶜāṣaba with the daughters
5 The son of a brother from the same father	is excluded by 8 categories:	the above 7 plus a full brother's son
6 The full father's brother	is excluded by 9 categories:	the above 8 plus the son of a brother from the same father
7 The father's brother from the same father	is excluded by 10 categories:	the above 9 plus a full father's brother's son
8 The full father's brother's son	is excluded by 11 categories:	the above 10 plus a father's brother from the same father
9 The father's brother's son from the same father	is excluded by 12 categories:	the above 11 plus a full father's brother's grandson

3.1.2.5.2 Three examples

After the general introduction (whole passages of which are given in shorter versions in the Official Gazette of the Republic of Yemen), one hundred practical examples of division of inheritance are given. Three such examples were selected:

It will be seen that – since inheritance calculations are admittedly not "easy" – the practical examples are supplemented by explanations and references and recalling the Koran and the Sharia – in a book destined for experts (identical copies were found in the offices of acting judges in Sana'a).

page 38
Problem 1
Justly solved

A man dies and leaves a father, a mother, a wife, one son, one daughter and 36 Dinar
The obligatory shares read:
1/6 the father,
1/6 the mother,
1/8 the wife,
and the rest goes to the son and daughter with the share of a man representing twice that of a female.

The solution by means of an arithmetic process is:

We prepare a table with the respective columns for the heirs entitled and their obligatory shares and the respective shares and the distributable legacy, and then enter the corresponding shares. We establish a common denominator (24)[108] for indicating the respective shares:

108 The common denominator here is 24; 1/6 = 4/24, 1/8 = 3/24, the denominator not being shown in the table.

The heirs and their obligatory shares	the shares 24/den.3		**tarika** 36/den.2		the respective amounts
1/6 : father	4		6		Dinar for father
1/6 : mother	4		6		Dinar for mother
1/8 : wife	3		4	1	Dinar for wife
Rest: son	8	2	13		Dinar for son
daughter	4	1	6	1	Dinar for daughter

And on the basis of the fundamental principle of the division of shares we now divide by the common denominator 24 in the calculation of the basic share of the legacy or calculation of the starting point. We then deduct the respective shares from the legacy, i.e.

24 : 6 = 4 shares for the father,
24 : 6 = 4 shares for the mother,
24 : 8 = 3 shares for the wife,

and this renders the remaining rest. We calculate this figure in terms of the common denominator 24, i.e. (the second principle):

4 + 4 + 3 = 11 shares for father, mother and wife,
24 - 11 = 13 shares for the son and the daughter,

and since twice the amount is due to the son than goes to the daughter we must establish their shares on the basis of three equal parts, i.e.
13 : 3 = 4 1/3 for the daughter,
4 1/3 times 2 = 8 2/3 for the son,

which renders a calculation in fractions so that yet another principle must be applied. We multiply the shares of each by 36 and divide by 24:

$$\frac{4 \text{ shares for the father} \cdot 36}{24} = 6 \text{ Dinar}$$

$$\frac{4 \text{ shares for the mother} \cdot 36}{24} = 6 \text{ Dinar}$$

$$\frac{3 \text{ shares for the wife} \cdot 36}{24} = 4\frac{1}{2} \text{ Dinar}$$

$$\frac{8\frac{2}{3} \text{ shares for the son} \cdot 36}{24} = 13 \text{ Dinar}$$

$$\frac{4\frac{1}{3} \text{ shares for the daughter} \cdot 36}{24} = 6\frac{1}{2} \text{ Dinar}$$

and this correct calculation is demonstrated in the above table
(6 + 6 + 4 1/2 + 13 + 6 1/2 = 36).

On page 58 we find a very simple example to show how easy a division can be:

Example 21

A man dies, leaving his wife, two granddaughters by his son, and a greatgrandson by his son.

The solution according to inheritance rules:
1/8 for the wife,
2/3 for the granddaughters,
and the rest goes to the greatgrandson, who is not **ʿasīb** with the granddaughters, because they are independent with their shares since he is lower in degree than they.
1/8 = 3/24
2/3 = 16/24
rest = 5/24

This is followed by a highly theoretical example which is announced as referring to a "blessed kinship" (and showing how a female profits from this):

Example 22

A man dies, leaving
a daughter,
a granddaughter by his son,
a greatgranddaughter by his son,
a greatgreatgranddaughter by his son,
a greatgreatgreatgranddaughter by his son,
and a daughter and a son who are children of his greatgreatgreatgreatgrandson,
and a granddaughter equivalent in degree but from a different father:

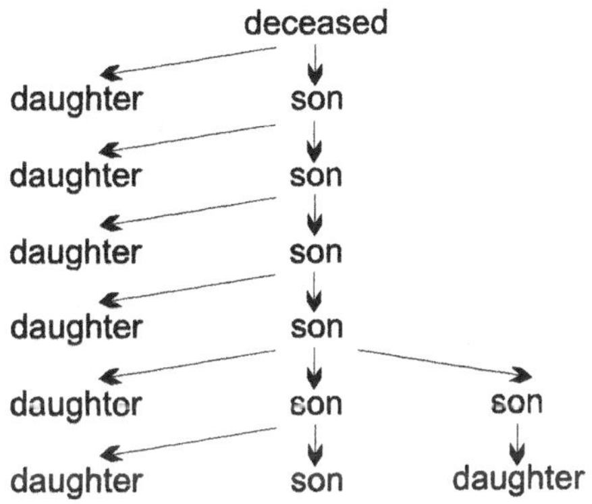

And the solution according to inheritance rules:

In this example the daughter of the son has an independent share and does not need to be **ᶜasaba** with the greatgrandson, and he is **ᶜasab** with his daughter and his father's brother's daughter, equivalent to him in degree and **ᶜasaba** with the father's sister and the grandfather's sister, so that she has a blessed kinship. And if he had already died, then the daughter and the granddaughter would inherit 2/3 and the rest would come to them again on the assumption that if there is no male, all the money will be for the daughters in the form of the obligatory shares and the distribution of the remainder.

1) If the male is in the first degree, the money would be shared between him and his sister (2/3 for him, 1/3 for her).

2) If the male is in the second degree, half is for the daughter and the rest for the grandson and his sister (2/6 and 1/6).

3) If the male is in the third degree, half would go to the daughters and 1/6 to the granddaughter, completing the 2/3, and the rest will be for the son and his daughter (2/3 and 1/3).

4) If the male is in the fourth degree, half would go to the daughter and 1/6 to the granddaughter, and the rest is for the son and his daughter and his father's sister.

5) If the male is in the fifth degree, half would go to the daughter and 1/6 to the granddaughter, and the rest goes to the two sons and their sister and their father's sister and their grandfather's sister.

6) If the male is in the sixth degree, half would go to the daughter and 1/6 to the granddaughter, and the rest is for the son and his daughter and his father's brother's sister who is equivalent to him in degree, and to his father's sister and his grandfather's sister and his greatgrandfather's sister.

And from this we learn that the grandson who is lower in degree according to **ᶜasabīya**[109] makes one or more sisters entitled to inherit, i.e. his father's brother's sister, equivalent to him in degree, his father's sister and further up to those who are higher in degree than he - and this can be used for the purpose of analogy.

When interviews were granted by judges employed at the Court in Sana'a, the above cited examples were submitted for comment or discussion. It was generally agreed that the procedure adopted followed the outline as recorded in the book quoted. But the fact was ever and again emphasised that if heirs agree to a different system of division, it will be accepted, that very often strict adherence to the above rules is not considered practical or beneficial, and that variations are devised and executed.

It was furthermore ascertained that women nowadays do go to court but not directly, they send a male representative. Two pending cases were disclosed, but (to the dismay of the interviewer) no judgment had as yet been passed, both cases being in such preliminary stages that nothing could be suggested as to the possible outcome..

109 For a comprehensive explanation of **ᶜaṣabīya** see Aziz Al-Azmeh: Ibn Khaldūn, 1993:29-31

3.1.2.5.3 A "generation model"

And in order to render the ever recurring references to "higher" and "lower" in degree, to nearer and farther representatives in the family pattern more lucid, the following table is given in terms of a "generation model" and the individual groups are numbered accordingly from 1 to 12:

Generation model

	former generations	
brothers and sisters of grandparents **11**	grandparents **5**	
brothers and sisters of parents **8**	parents **3**	children of brothers and sisters of grandparents **12**
brothers and sisters **6**	EGO and spouse **1**	children of brothers and sisters of parents **10**
	children **2**	children of brothers and sisters **7**
	grandchildren **4**	grandchildren of brothers and sisters **9**
	further generations	

3.1.2.6 Yemen legal gazettes

For a modern version of all these laws the respective legal texts as published in the Official Gazette[110] of the Republic of Yemen were consulted. As will be seen, the individual articles adhere almost literally to the wording as found in the Koran and the Sharia.

Resolution of the Republic concerning Law No. 20 /1992

Article 307

In accordance with this law the following 6 categories have a claim to the estate of a deceased, and this in the following order:

1. Main heirs, or those entitled to a fixed share (**aṣḥāb al-farūḍ**):
   1) the daughters and the son's daughters and the female children of the latter,
   2) the full sisters,
   3) the sisters on the father's side (same father),
   4) the mother,
   5) the brothers or sisters by the same mother,
   6) the spouse,
   7) the mother's or the father's grandmother,
   8) the father or the father's father or the one before him (the father's grandfather).

2. Heirs not entitled to a fixed share (**ᶜaṣabāt al-nisbīya**):

   1) male: the son, the son's son and the male child of the latter,
   the father and the father's father and the one before him,
   the full brother, the father's (half) brother, the full brother's son and his sons, the father's (half) brother's son and his sons, the full father's brother, the father's (half) brother from the father's side, the full father's brother's son and his male children.

   2) female: the daughters and the son's daughters,
   the full sisters, the sisters from the father's side,
   all the above if there is no male equivalent.

---

110 Official Gazette of the Republic of Yemen, No. 20/1992

3. Every relative not entitled to a fixed share and not an ᶜāṣab (**d̲ū ar-raḥm**).

4. A relative legitimised by a declaration (**al-maqar lahu binasib**).

5. Someone getting more than the one third (in the will) if there is no-one entitled to inherit, i.e. if there is no Koranic heir (**al-mawsī lahu akt̲ar min al-t̲ult̲ ḥait̲u lā wārit̲**).[111]

6. The mortmain (**bait al-māl**).

Article 308

The division is effected in the following way:
One half, one quarter, one eighth, two thirds, one third, one sixth.

Article 309

The following five have a claim to 1/2:
1) the husband, if the deceased has no next of kin entitled to inherit,
2) an only daughter if there is no male equivalent,
3) the son's only daughter, if there is no male equivalent,
4) an only full sister, if she is not excluded,
5) an only (half) sister on the father's side.

Article 310

The following 3 have a claim to 1/3:
1) the husband, if the deceased has next of kin entitled to inheritance,
2) the wife or the wives, if the deceased has no next of kin entitled to inheritance,
3) the mother in the case of inheritance for the wife and the parents.

Article 311

1/8 is the share of the wife or the wives, if the deceased has next of kin entitled to inheritance.

---

111 If someone has no Koranic heirs he may in his will bequeath more than one third to someone else

Article 312

2/3 go to the following:
1) two daughters or more, if there is no male equivalent,
2) two or more son's daughters, if there is no male equivalent and if they are not excluded,
3) two or more full sisters, if there is no male equivalent,
4) two or more sisters from the father's side, if they are not excluded.

Article 313

1/3 go to the following two:
1) the mother, if the deceased has no next of kin entitled to inherit and if there is no brother and no sister,
2) two or more mother's brothers, if the deceased has no male children, taking into consideration that if the mother has one or more full brothers these are entitled to claim their share in this 1/3.

Article 314

1/6 may be claimed by the following:
1) the father, if not excluded,
2) the true grandfather, if not excluded,
3) the mother, if the deceased has next of kin entitled to inherit, or two or more brothers or sisters with a spouse or parents,
4) the son's daughter or more of them together with the only daughter share 2/3, if there is no male equivalent,
5) the father's half sister or more of them together with an only full sister share 2/3, if she inherits,
6) the mother's half brother or half sister, if there is only one and the deceased has no next of kin entitled to inherit and there are no male children,
7) the grandmother or grandmothers, if they are not excluded.

Article 322
ḥujb

There are two kinds of **ḥujb**:
1) reduction,
2) prevention.

This is a different method of calculating claims, but the result for those concerned is the same - as will be seen:

Article 323

Reduction is limited to five shareholders:

- a husband's share is reduced from 1/2 to 1/4 if there are children or grand-children,
- a wife's or wives' shares are reduced from 1/4 to 1/8 if there are children or grandchildren,
- a mother's share is reduced from 1/3 to 1/6 by children or two or more brothers and/or sisters, even if they do not inherit, and a mother's share of 1/3 of the estate may be reduced to 1/3 of the rest by the presence of another spouse of the father,
- the son's daughter's share is reduced from 1/2 to 1/6 if there is a daughter, and if there are more of them, from 2/3 to 1/6,
- a sister's share (from the father only) is reduced from 1/2 to 1/6 if there is a full sister, and if there are more than one, from 2/3 to 1/6.

Article 324

Prevention affects the following 11:

This text fully corresponds to the **ḥujb** table given above, but as the table is divided into one section for group 1 and another for group 2, 6 and 12 categories are given to cover all the heirs involved. What might be considered a minor repetition in the outlay of the table makes the overall presentation much more obvious and easier for consultation.

3.1.2.7 A detailed questionnaire discussed with imams

For the purpose of checking the information obtained from documents and legal texts, a questionnaire was prepared and submitted to two imams of mosques, one a Zaidi and the other a Shafi'i.

In this context it may be of interest to learn how this information was obtained. Imams of mosques may be fairly easily accessible for men who see them when they go to the mosque. A woman has two possible methods of approach. She either asks a man to pass on her request to the imam and try to arrange a meeting outside the mosque, or she tries to find out where the imam lives and attempts to gain admission to his house by contacting the ladies there and asking for their intervention. To find out where an imam lives is not difficult. The children who play in all of the streets and thus also in front of every mosque will not only tell you, they will insist on accompanying you there. To be admitted into the house is less easy. You have to shout who you are, why you want to enter, what you want to know. To explain to a person behind closed shutters two floors higher than ground level why a European woman, not a Muslim, wants to present the imam with a questionnaire she wants to take back home, could be regarded as a somewhat unusual form of negotiation.

Yet the project as prepared by the interviewer materialised. In each case the lady of the house was prepared to take charge of the questionnaire, drafted in as calligraphic an Arabic as the writer could muster, and hand it over to the imam for him to decide whether he would be willing to discuss and/or answer it. The interviewer was asked to return one day later at a certain hour.

When she did so she was admitted without delay, in each case the questionnaires had already been filled in and signed, and the imams were ready to discuss any further questions. It should also be mentioned that in both cases the imams had learned friends sitting with them who participated in the conversation.

The questionnaire and the respective answers are given in a translation on the following pages to permit direct comparison:

Questions submitted to a zaidi and a shafi'i Imam	*zaidi Imam*	*shafi'i Imam*
1. What is the percentage of zaidites in Sana'a and who else is represented?	Try to find the percentage yourself. We do not have any statistics	Zaidites are from Yarim to Sa'da and the rest of the country is shafi'i, and nothing else matters
2. What is the difference between zaidi and shafi'i?	The mut^ca-marriage is not allowed for zaidites	The difference between zaidi and shafi'i is like the difference between sky and earth and they disagree in all matters
3. What are the sources of law?	As quoted in the respective literature	The **uṣūl al-fiqh** are always a part and a form of the Sharia, are independent and cannot differ
4. What are the sources of law applied in Sana'a?	**šarh al-azhār**	(Also) zaidi rule of thought is included in **šarh al-azhār** and other supporting writing, and some rules are selected from the four sunni sects
5. What is the difference between the different schools of law in respect to inheritance?	There is agreement in most matters as far as inheritance is concerned	There is no difference between the sects in inheritance matters because Allah has specified all this in the **sūrat an-nisa'**. There are some minor things which they disagree on but these are not important
6. And if all items are specified in the law, what is the role of [c]**urf**? And is the latter common knowledge passed on by word of mouth?	[c]**urf** is alright if it is not against Sharia, otherwise not	Sharia is not affected by [c]**urf** since this or any other tribal law must not violate Sharia. These are just habits

7. Is it correct to assume that people do not go to court in matters of inheritance as long as the family relationship is a good one (they try to settle amicably if at all possible)?	Inheritance is divided by the God of the people and you have nothing else to do but to follow what he says in his book	This seems likely but as time passes and habits change ... If a division were not done by a judge those affected might claim revision years later ...
8. Does a person inheriting a share pay taxes?	No	There are no expenses or charges except those you pay for the division and for the people who make the evaluation
9. And if a person dies and leaves debts and nothing to inherit?	Debts need only be paid if there is something left. But voluntary payments are accepted on the idea that the dead person would profit from this vis-à-vis Allah	No one is forced to pay debts – if you do so, this is considered a charity
10. And if there is only a house left, who gets it?	See as stated in literature (3 above)	No one is allowed to claim a house in the case of debts unless all the legacy are debts – then the heir has the choice of paying the debts or parting with the house
11. And if a father dies, is the son obliged to pay his debts?	No	See 12
12. And if a son dies, is the father obliged to pay his debts?	No	Neither is obliged, unless there is something left. But if the son has made debts in the father's name, the father would have to pay

13.	And the son's son inherits in Yemen?	If a man dies and has children, they inherit and nothing is for the son of the son, unless the grandfather has written a will for him, to include him among his father's brothers and sisters in case the father died while the grandfather was alive. But he is not entitled to more than a third.	The son's son only inherits if there is no son, and if he gets anything in the presence of father's brothers, then only if this is accepted by them
14.	And the son's daughter?	This holds true also for the daughter of a son	She gets nothing
15.	Is there a special particularity in Yemen that the son's son inherits in the presence of a father's brother?	This is the division of Allah	As I said before, only if accepted by the heirs
16.	Some people keep telling me that women sometimes never get any **mahr** before getting divorced. Is that true? And what happens if the husband dies? And if a woman has given her **mahr** to her husband to build a house or start a business, and the husband dies, what happens then?	The woman has the right to ask for her **mahr** on the day of marriage, and if payment is delayed to the death of the husband, this is not correct in accordance with Sharia	This refers to a system in some of the villages as a bond between two partners. But something must be given before the man gets together with his wife*, such as a necklace, silver or gold or amber, and this as a symbol in accordance with what is stated in Sharia. And if the husband dies, the woman gets her entire **mahr**, and if she dies, her **mahr** will be divided between her heirs. But the woman can give her **mahr** to her husband by way of a present or as a loan. (Koran cited: Verse 3 of Chapter on women) * (as a gesture when the veil is lifted)

17.	And who decides on munāsik̲a?	No answer	If the **tarika** has not been divided for generations and someone asks for the division, then division takes place, but it is a long process to establish each share
18.	What is the present provision in line with the Constitution as regards female judges? How many female judges do exist?	If anyone has been working hard and has achieved benefits, he or she is entitled to become what he or she wants	No answer
19.	According to Islamic thinking a man gets twice as much as a woman. And this since the man is required to provide for the women in his family. But there are women now who work and need no longer be supported by a man. Will the law change and specify that men and women get equal shares?	No	Allah has said that since a man always has a family to look after (parents, brothers, sisters, wife, children) while women are not supposed to be on their own, but either have a family to look after them or, if they are alone, are only they themselves and thus 1/2 suffices
20.	A special case: a man dies and leaves a daughter who is not married and has no job. Why is she not given everything her father leaves?	If a man dies leaving daughters and a son's son, the daughters get 2/3 and the son's son the rest. If there is only 1 daughter she gets 1/2 and the rest is for the son's son	She gets 1/2 and this is already much in comparison with a man – as I stated before

The information provided in the foregoing text and to be read from the documents quoted was confirmed by the answers to the questions listed and can be summed up as follows:

- There are no data on percentages of religious sects represented in Sana'a.
- The souces of law as applied in Sana'a are Koran and Sharia as quoted in the documents referred to.
- As far as inheritance is concerned there is no essential difference between the sects.
- No taxes are payable.
- The payment of debts in the absence of a legacy is voluntary.
- The legal provision with regard to inheritance in favour of the son's children as promulgated in Decision No. 24/1986 and revoked and abrogated in 1992[112] may have been repudiated by the **ʿulamāʾ** on the grounds of not corresponding to Sharia.
- The half share of a woman is strictly maintained.

112 ibid:63

3.1.2.8 A questionnaire submitted to the Mufti

As reported and described it had not been too difficult to meet the imams and obtain first-hand information from them. Upon further consideration another very short questionnaire was elaborated to be submitted to the Mufti. It would, of course, not have been wise to go to the Mufti's office on one of the official reception days and mingle with the high-ranking, exclusively male guests waiting for admittance. The author begged a niece of the Mufti, whom she had already met on several occasions, to help her think of a suitable way of approach. She was shortly afterwards contacted by the husband of this friend who asked for the questionnaire as his wife had instructed him that this was an important matter to be brought before the Mufti without delay.

The Mufti fell ill and daily bulletins on his state of health were broadcast. He did not recover before the departure of the researcher. However, she received a message from the Mufti's office to leave a fax number for further reference. Three months later a fax arrived with the completed questionnaire, handwritten, signed and sealed by the Mufti and including his very best wishes for a successful termination of the study.

MUFTI QUESTIONNAIRE
Answers (in **bold**)

1. What are the respective percentages of zaidis and shafi'is (in Sana'a) – approximately?

   In Sana'a there is a zaidi majority but no one can give exact numbers.

2. Which law is applied by judges in Sana'a?

   In Sana'a zaidi law is applied, which has a number of particularities as regards purchasing contracts. There was also a special feature regarding wills, but this no longer applies.

3. What is the difference between the zaidi school of law and sunna in inheritance matters?

   No difference.

   And this on the assumption that the zaidis do not consider themselves a branch of shi'a,

   zaidis are a sect of their own (following Ali and in this respect following the religious line of the shi'a), are nearest of all to sunna, are more moderate

   and, consequently, what is the difference between zaidi and shi'i in inheritance matters?

   There are substantial differences in inheritance matters – zaidi inheritance is not shi'i.

4. What are the sources of law?

   The respective literature as quoted by the imams.

5. How are **qudā'** appointed and what rules apply?

   By the ministry of justice (prime minister).

6. How is the relationsship between the **ᶜulamā'** at the mosques and the appointed professors at the University (at the department for Sharia and law and for Islamic studies)?

   Studying Sharia law at the university is now obligatory. Some study at the university and then study for some time at a mosque.

7. What is your personal opinion as regards **ᶜurf**? I was told that **ᶜurf** is applied for the solution of many problems and only a few are settled according to Sharia.

   ᶜurf must be compatible with Sharia.

3.2 Section B – Selected aspects of the legal system

Since this study is concerned with women's inheritance a number of issues require more special attention:

3.2.1 A note on the female share

A survey of general Islamic literature may easily lead to the conclusion that a female invariably receives a half share only as opposed to the full share of a man. But this proves inaccurate. The uterine sister inherits equally with her brother, and so does a mother with the father of a deceased. It is the daughter and the sister from the father's side who receive only half as much as their male counterparts if they inherit jointly.

The case of the wife is particularly interesting. Her share is one half of the share the husband would inherit from her were he the survivor. The full implication of this provision must be seen in the light of the fact that the husband and the wife hold their properties and possessions independently of each other; but the Muslim husband usually owns more than his wife and is therefore likely to leave more behind than would the wife. If he inherits from the wife, although his share is bigger than her share would be, he will receive, comparatively speaking, much less than the wife receives with a smaller share in a bigger property.

In Islam, women are free from economic responsibilities. They are not legally required to provide for any person, not even for themselves. They are fully maintained by male relatives. Even the wealthy wife must be maintained by the husband, the sister by the brother, the mother by the son, the daughter by the father, etc. These obligations to relatives may well exceed what a male could possibly inherit from them. If then a larger share of the property is allocated to the exclusively liable male, who may be responsible for an entire household or even beyond, and a smaller share is allocated to the economically non-responsible female(s), the allocation cannot be called discrimination against women.

In the imagery of the Muslim scholar this may even read as follows:[113]

"The Muslim woman, by receiving a smaller share of the property than the man's, is not in fact being denied the fruits of any effort on her part or the produce of any

113 ᶜAbd al 'Ati, Hammudah: The Family Structure in Islam, 1977:270

of her labour. It is not that she earned something which is being withheld or taken away from her. Whatever she takes of the property of the deceased relative is in return for nothing material she has done or contributed. She inherits out of compassion or kindness, and not because she has discharged or will discharge any financial duty to any relative. Even the few jurists who held a woman with means responsible for the support of needy kin stipulated, in one interpretation, that her share of the burden be only according to her share of inheritance. If she joins her brother in the support of a needy father, she will bear one third of the cost, while he bears two thirds, just as if they were sharing the father's estate."

It can be assumed that the author of the above text is not aware of the contributions women make and have made to the well-being or pure survival of a family without any property being accumulated or duty discharged. It must be assumed that he has not yet had access to information on the growing number of matrifocal families – many of them in third world countries.

3.2.2 A note on mahr (dower, bridal money)

Since **mahr** appears to be a subject of perpetual disagreement among researchers, and a field of glaring contradictions and clashing opinions, and will be an item discussed in all the interviews in Part Two, it was considered imperative to first study an official source of information, the respective chapter in the Law Gazette:[114]

Chapter Two

Article 33

1. **mahr** must be given to a woman getting married in line with a valid contract, and it refers to what has been agreed upon in terms of money or property as specified, and if this is not specified or no longer remembered, the woman must be given a similar amount as the other women.

2. **mahr** is the property of the woman and she can do whatever she likes with it, and no other conditions apply.

---

114 **al-qarār al-jumhūrīy bi-l-qānūn raqm** 20/1992: Chapter Two

Article 34.

All or part of the **mahr** may be given immediately or may be delayed, but if the delay is not accepted by the woman she is entitled to claim it at any time.

Article 35.

Mahr becomes due to the full extent upon consummation of a marriage and must be paid/given upon the death of either of the marriage partners.

Article 36.

Half the **mahr** specified is due upon divorce or separation if wanted by the husband before consummation of the marriage; but if wanted by both sides or by the woman only, no **mahr** is due, and the woman is obliged to return what she has received as **mahr**; but if she has already made contributions to her husband out of her **mahr**, she need not give more than what is left.

Article 37.

If a woman's **mahr** has not been specified correctly and she is divorced before consummation of the marriage, she is entitled to a benefit which is an outfit of a comparable woman of a comparable man, but this benefit must not exceed half of the **mahr** of a comparable woman.

Article 38.

A deceived/wronged/victimised woman is entitled to the **mahr** of a comparable woman.

Article 39.

A woman may refuse consummation of marriage until her **mahr** has been specified and paid, unless part of it was agreed to be delayed for a specified period or according to **ʿurf**, in which case she must not refuse intercourse before the end of this period; and all this must be seen in the context of what is stated in Article 34.

It would appear appropriate to render some explanations obtained in the field as to the meaning of the above text:

- "no longer remembered" refers to the fact that a marriage contract may be orally agreed upon so that the witnesses might forget;

- "the woman must be given a similar amount" refers to the accepted practice of keeping **mahr** at a comparable level for all women of a family, a community, a class;

- the same applies to the outfit of a comparable woman, and "outfit" refers to an entire set of dresses, gowns, headwear, underwear, shoes, cosmetics, including perfumes, a prayer rug, etc. or all the items that would be found in the trousseau of a woman of that class.

For the purpose of inheritance the vital passage is Article 35. The stipulation of the **mahr** becoming due upon the death of either marriage partner is to be understood to mean that if the husband dies, the woman is entitled to immediate reception of her **mahr** without this being part of the husband's estate. The **mahr** represents one of the debts that must be paid before division of inheritance can take place. When the woman then dies, the **mahr** is considered part of what she leaves and is divided accordingly.

From the above it becomes obvious why in Islam the idea of bequeathing a particular item in a woman's possession to a particular member of the family does not follow the western pattern. The woman is not supposed to make a will in favour of Koranic heirs, while on the other hand she might not want to give something away while still alive and not knowing how long she would live. She has to leave it to the agreement between her survivors whether or not they accept what she might have suggested or wished them to do after her death.

Before discussing possible applications or economic cycles of a mahr, a short summary of relevant reflections appears appropriate.[115]

The **mahr** is that part of payment for a wife which is destined for the bride/woman herself – as in contrast to the **šarṭ** which is paid to the father for (among other matters) arranging the wedding, and reimbursing him for previous expenses. As regards the amount of a **mahr**, nearly all authors who have treated the subject agree that official stipulations should be considered as guidelines only. In actual fact every woman asked will give a statement of her own of how her **mahr** was

---

115 See also Mansour, Fahmy: La condition de la femme dans la tradition et l'évaluation de l'islamisme, 1913:143 bis

calculated. Gerholm[116] suggests that a plausible assumption could be that a small **mahr** is given in poorer families, where both sides lack money and the wife renders as much unpaid work as she can to contribute to the living of the family, and the **mahr** is viewed more or less as a small recognition, whereas rich brides are given impressive sums to underline their better standing. But since the purpose of a **mahr** is also seen as one way of safeguarding the wife's future in the case of a divorce one might infer that the poor woman is expected to manage in the absence of a **mahr** while the rich one will be comfortably positioned as before.

To put this theoretical reasoning into a practical frame, let us summarise authentic examples:

A man would like to divorce his wife but is reluctant to pay her **mahr**. Since the **mahr** should have been provided for as he is supposed to have furnished it at the time of marrying - while the poor man who promises to create a **mahr** successively is the exception to the rule – he either parts with the **mahr** or negotiates with his wife. If the wife wants to be divorced, she might be willing to forego her **mahr** to obtain her freedom. The underlying economic consideration is that the man who wants to divorce and parts with the **mahr** no longer needs this money to support his wife. Should he want to remarry, he will be able to do so only if he can find the money for a second **mahr**, unless the wife wants to be divorced because she would like to marry someone else who would be able and ready to support her, so that she might not need her **mahr**.

As far as inheritance is concerned, a **mahr** can only be "inherited" where a husband died before giving it to a wife. And as is stated above, this **mahr** is then considered a debt due to the wife – and she does not get it as inheritance! If the woman dies leaving her husband behind, the **mahr** belongs automatically to the husband and is no longer due. If a mother dies a widow, the **mahr**, with all other property left, is divided according to the provisions of the Koran.

In this context yet another variation must be referred to. Above all in modern times women very often resolve to use the **mahr** to give the family a start. Thus, in order to enable the husband to start a business or buy a house, the woman contributes her **mahr**. If she does so without making sure that legal documents are drawn up she can easily be confronted with a situation where her husband dies and she is not

116 Gerholm, Tomas: Aspects of Inheritance and Marriage Payments in North Yemen, 1985:138 bis

reimbursed for her previous contribution. If she has documents she can insist that the equivalent of her **mahr** be subtracted from the **tarika** before the division takes place.

Where the **mahr** consists of jewels and/or gold, there are sometimes tacit agreements that before division these items are passed on to daughters without being considered part of the legacy.

And yet another fact was pointed out in the course of the research. For the sake of equal standing some families make sure that **mahr** is the same for all female members among them. A father will expect a son-in-law to give the same **mahr** to his daughter as the father's sister received when she got married – "so that there will be no competition" (personal communication).

A very interesting situation is referred to in the information supplied by an old man talking about the time when he was young:

"In those days men had only one **futa** (skirt) and women only one dress. My uncle also told me that there was one nice dress in the village that every bride borrowed to wear for her wedding, and the village owned three Maria Theresia thalers that would be given to each bride as her **mahr**, but she had to return them." (Taken from a textbook for elementary school)

3.2.3 A note on munāsika̱ (postponement of the division of inheritance)

A subject very little referred to and, if so, in rather general terms not yielding any detailed information[117], but for which a number of practical examples were encountered during the research, is the phenomenon of voluntary postponement of inheritance, which at first sight admittedly appears somewhat unexpected.

Yemeni law stipulates[118], very casually, that:

Munāsika̱ means that one or more of the heirs of a deceased person die(s) before a division (of the estate) is made. When the division is eventually effected, it cannot

117 Mundy, Martha: Female Inheritance in Highland Yemen, 1976:176

118 Art. 347 in Yemeni Gazette No. 20/1992

be done without dividing the first **tarika** before proceeding with the second, i.e. it is obligatory that the division be accomplished in two parts.

These parts are explained in the legal text, but the explanation given and the example quoted by the Hanafitic School and shown in Section A are much more practical and illustrative.

The real importance of **munāsika** may not be obvious from the text as such. Besides the intriguing aspect of the difficulties involved in a division according to Islamic law, and how long it takes for an heir to be able to really avail himself of a share[119], attention must be paid to the practical aspects involved in a division:

A costly and long-winded procedure will be necessary to establish who gets what. Heirs are obliged to negotiate and renegotiate before being able to actually enjoy the benefits of their new wealth. It may very often prove much more practical – and profitable – to leave a **tarika** intact and only share the accruing profit.

3.2.4 A note on orphans, handicapped children and elopers

(Specific reference to orphans, handicapped children and elopers may appear to be a rather general item when expressly dealing with female inheritance. It was found, though, that orphans, but also handicapped children of the female sex, are sometimes even more disadvantaged than their male counterparts in terms of access to schools and medical treatment, but also in terms of receiving equal treatment by their guardians managing their property. While with elopers it is somewhat intriguing that it is always the girl who is referred to as having taken to such questionable devices while the young man involved seems to be magically transposed onto foreign territory.)

Verses 2, 5, 6 and 7 of Surat an-Nisa' clearly refer to Allah's instructions as to the treatment of orphans. Verse 11 explicitly states what will happen to those cheating them out of their inheritance. Verse 4 stipulates that those of "weak intellect" should not be given their property but should be looked after.

As far as orphans are concerned, there is common agreement that a guardian be appointed until they come of age. Their shares are as provided for according to their position in the kinship pattern. The guardian is expected to manage their inheritance

119 Gerholm, Tomas, 1985:131

as best he can. If he fails to do so or does not act in the interest and to the benefit of his wards he not only loses credibility as a good Muslim, he can and will also be brought to trial.

Neither the Koran, nor the law, nor public opinion make any difference between orphans and those of "weak intellect" nor, for that matter, disabled persons. The two latter categories are considered dependents whether minors or not.

In this context mention must be made of the different attitude of Muslims towards both mentally and physically disabled persons. They are never excluded or hidden but remain within the family or the community. In the same way as old or ailing persons are considered full members of the family, incapacitated beings are also fully integrated. In her stories about the life of women in Yemen[120], Nagiba gives touching accounts of how naturally people behave towards those with physical or mental deficiencies. The idea of abandoning an old parent by leaving him or her in a "home" horrifies Yemenis. The same applies to handicapped children. Looking after them is considered a fulfilment of Allah's will.

As far as an orphan's property is concerned, to return to the aspect of inheritance, the above is a statement of "how it should be". Flagrant cases of disobedience to Allah's will are notorious. Guardians not supervised by other members of the family (who sometimes can be relied on to do so in their very own interest) very often either attempt to retain an unfair share of their wards' property on the pretext of being entitled to remuneration for their expenses, or try to postpone the transfer of property on the pretext that the ward even when of age should accept further guidance, and this particularly in the case of female wards.

In the "awkward" event of a girl eloping and emigrating to another country with the husband of her choice, who is not accepted by the family, and of the two marrying there, the difficulty of establishing whether or not she inherits is a purely practical one (and the same holds true for the young man).

There is no doubt that elopers also are entitled to their shares since no provision to the contrary can be quoted from the Koran. However, those having left Yemen secretly, and in all probability without having left a forwarding address, would have to know about the death in the family back home to be able to return at the time the division is made. If they are absent they may be referred to as "missing or lost" and

---

120 Fayein, Claudie: Vies de femmes au Yémen, Récits de Nagiba, 1990: Chapter V

their shares either passed on to those entitled to inherit from them or deposited with someone else who may not be so very eager to inform them.

3.3 A final summarising note

Whenever the subject of inheritance is referred to in the presence of Muslims, or, for the purpose of this study, Yemeni Muslims, the Koran is quoted. And this not only with regard to the subject matter as such, for instance the respective shares, the provisions proper, but very much also in respect of the attitude, the behaviour, the expectations, the spontaneous reactions manifested by anyone addressed on the subject.

May it be permitted to reflect on a fundamental difference between Muslims and non-Muslims also in their contrasting approaches to scientific discoveries. In times of breathtaking technological achievements the western expert postulates a discovery in terms of scientific knowledge, based on evidence supported by acknowledged data. The Muslim scientist will be satisfied with a discovery only upon having found the compatibility of modern processes with the undisputable, overriding principles laid down in the Koran. This was successfully accomplished after the first landing on the moon, and also as far as the use of atomic energy is concerned. Thus there is every reason to expect that in the event of compelling developments the respective passages permitting a somewhat different interpretation of inheritance, not only in general but also in respect of women, will be found in the Koran.

4. Part Two

4.1 Jurisprudence and sociology

This study is intended to compare documented rules with reality, to contrast legal texts with actual circumstances and cases encountered or referred to. This will therefore also be a comparison of laws established in jurisprudence with findings obtained or available in sociology.

One might postulate that jurisprudence as a dogmatic science concentrates on "how it should be", laying down provisions, specifications and standards and creating the instrumentarium for implementing it, while sociology is concerned with the description and explanation of "how it is".[121] This in turn gives rise to consideration of the probability of reasonable interaction between the two criteria. Laws are not created in a void, they are formulated in an existing society, are drafted to meet a manifested demand for regulations. The legislator will only be in a position to promulgate a useful law if he has a fair knowledge of the society he creates it for. The "law-abiding citizen" will meet the expectations of a legal theory in the long run only if this theory is based on reality-oriented parameters.

Ethnosociologists have opined that it is impossible to define law as such since "it is inseparably connected with the culture of a people".[122] Rules are drafted to reflect standard behaviour. The behaviour demonstrated by the majority of a society will be or become a standard. The importance or implications of a rule will be understandable only in the context of the social pattern it is applied to.

But laws are made by lawyers and are interpreted and applied by lawyers. They are bound to accommodate much more to "sophisticated" needs of the upper classes than to conflicting interests of the lower classes. Only very few judges stem from the lower strata of society. It will be discussed later how this affects attitudes and actions of the individual in a society.

---

121 Girtler, Roland: Rechtssoziologie – Thesen und Möglichkeiten, 1976:15, 16

122 Hoebel, E.A.: The Law of Primitive Men, 1964:29

As Martha Munday[123] states, the practice of inheritance cannot be read from the legal text, but demands analysis of the institutions of the law. Once we abandon the simple notion of the practice of law as immediate enforcement of a text, we may be more inclined to observe that farā'iḍ law defines the social pattern of inheritance and yet is only rarely carried out to the letter. It is not a question of the failure of the law as an intellectual process, but of the complex institutional mediation between text and practice.

Thus the ideology of inheritance exists almost independently of the outcome in particular cases of inheritance. The practices of dividing property seldom correspond to the partition prescribed by the law. Yet the law determines the very framework within which negotiations concerning the devolution of property are pursued.

4.2 Social structure

For an examination of the sociology of the Islamic law of inheritance the developments in the recent past should be reviewed.

In order to do so, the social structure must be referred to. This appears to be of much more importance to foreign observers than to the population. Those born there or having become integrated into Yemeni society find the subject of but minor importance, class disputes or status arguments are rarely encountered. Foreign observers, though, have paid particular attention to the status hierarchy.[124]

Essentially, most authors see Yemeni society as divided into a hierarchy of strata, but they differ to some extent over the number of constituent status groups by which these are ranked. The system still encountered shortly after the revolution has, in any event, been changing under the impact of rapidly altering economic circumstances and new ideological influences. The traditional conventional ranking according to Meissner would read:

"1) sādah (pl. of sayyid): The descendants of the Prophet Muhammad through the union of his daughter Fathimah with his cousin ᶜAli. The Zaidi Imam was,

123 Munday, Martha: Modern Interpretation of the Islamic Law of Inheritance, 1988:50, 51

124 Meissner, Jeffrey R.: Tribes at the Core: Legitimacy, Structure and Power in Zaidi Yemen, 1987:126 bis

thus, a sayyid. By virtue of their descent from the Prophet's tribe, Quraysh, the sadah are descendants of ᶜAdnān, ancestor of the Northern Arabs.

2) qabayil (pl. of qabīli): "tribesmen". They are free, arm-bearing men of honorable status, and supplied the bulk of the Imam's military support. Most of them claim a common Southern Arab (Qahtāni) ancestry.

3) mazayanah (pl. of muzayyin): free men of low status. Many of them follow occupations regarded as dishonorable according to "tribal" values. They are (or were) regarded as being without honor and of unknown ancestry.

Two further groups, represented by a much smaller proportion of the population, are:

- akhdām (pl. of khadim, meaning literally "servants"), and
- ᶜabīd (pl. of ᶜabd), ex-slaves and their descendants."

The first two groups, Meissner goes on to explain in more detail, the "sādah" and the "qabāyil", are alike in claiming known, honourable ancestry. The third category (and others, who may be assimilated with them) by definition lack both honourable descent and honour. The possession of a particular social status, membership in a particular social category, to some extent determines a person's occupation (some occupations are honourable, some neutral, some "dishonouring") and the range of marriage choices open to him (or her).

The third group may be defined negatively – as comprising those who are neither "sādah" nor "qabāyil", who are without known ancestry (**nasab**) and honour (**šaraf**), and did not bear arms or hold political power. To a certain extent, it can also be seen as a residual category: foreigners – Muslims from other countries who settled in Yemen – were most easily assimilated into this category.

This third status category may, however, also be defined positively, in terms of economic functions that persons within it fill. Butchering, barbering, inn-keeping and other occupations which the tribesmen regard as dishonourable are practised exclusively by the "mazayanah", although persons of this status were not generally restricted to such occupations. The "mazayanah" are, one may say, the "invisible" people in Yemeni history, they are rarely mentioned in historical accounts. There are a number of other terms for this group: **ahl al-k̲ums, banū al-k̲ums, ahl al-t̲ult̲, bayyaᶜ, ᶜanādil, nuqqas**.

The **akdām** are a black population of African origin. The theory that they are of Ethiopian origin is still the common view in Yemen. Many of them live as scavengers, sweepers or beggars on the margin of society. But there are also larger groups of them practising the same occupations as the "mazayanah", operating hostels and restaurants.

The **ʿabīd**, ex-slaves and their descendants, are mostly of obvious African origin. Slaves were being brought into Yemen from East Africa as late as the 1920s and 1930s. Some, however, are light-skinned and are not physically distinguishable from the majority of the population. Their social ranking is somewhat difficult to assess. They are sometimes regarded as the lowest possible stratum, while others grant them honour. They do not share the occupations of the **akdām**. And a **qabīli** may well marry a woman of such origin.

The above social system has in the meantime become almost history. It has been subjected to essential changes, to be attributed to, and explained by, two circumstances:

a) the great number of migrants who left Yemen and became wealthy abroad. On returning to their country they have created other status forms and values and have, among other things, also become preferred marriage partners.

b) with the opening of the country following the revolution and the growing number of students receiving university education in the West, the traditional patterns have started to disintegrate. A great number of sons of "qabayil" have obtained university degrees in the United States of America and have started businesses in Sana'a their fathers would never have considered a proper source of income.

In discussions with Yemenis, the question of social classes was considered to be altogether out of date (except, of course, as far as the **sāda** are concerned). It was even suggested that the definition be accepted that only two categories exist: the **akdām** and all others. And it was specially pointed out that even in the case of the **akdām** changes are accepted. A singer used to be a very low person indeed, but so many of them have risen to very highly respected positions, earn fabulous incomes and are immensely popular and appreciated that now they are fully accepted by the young (while the older generation still hesitate).

It is interesting to see how a Yemeni lawyer[125] refers to the classification of social groups by quoting a renowned Yemeni source (Abu Ghanem), and reassuring to find minor diversions only:

" (a) sheikhs of tribes;
(b) sadah, jurists and judges
(c) important men and tribesmen;
(d) professionals and artisans;
(e) those with demeaning occupations, like barbers, blacksmiths, blood-letters, butchers, circumcisers, green-grocers, musicians and others under the plethora of other names."

And Al-Hubaishi goes on to say that although he agrees with Abu Ghanem's assertion that those are social ranks, levels or categories and not classes in an economic sense, nevertheless those ranks are idioms of social inequality.

The above is of particular significance also for the eligibility considerations in respect of marriage candidates and, consequently, family and kinship. A study of women's issues would not be complete without due reference to the systems and customs of marriage arrangements.

4.3 Marriage arrangements

In order to meet classical anthropological stipulations, the aspect of the overriding importance of the **bint al-ᶜamm** (father's brother's daughter) is here referred to. Whenever the subject was raised in discussions with informants, **bint al-ᶜamm** was agreed to be the favoured bride since this meant that the family property would stay together. But, as women pointed out, such a bride might just as well be considered to come from the mother's side and thus represent another type of relationship. It is, of course, not the relationship which is different, but the way of viewing or terming it. Since this study is concerned with women it is suggested family patterns should be viewed from the women's point of view too and some literature meeting this purpose quoted and analysed. A beautiful example is demonstrated by Bourdieu[126], referring to the two possible modes of viewing one and the same relationship. A classificatory parallel cousin might just as well be a maternal cross cousin:

---

125 Al-Hubaishi, H.A.: Legal System and Basic Law in Yemen, 1988:63

126 Bourdieu, Pierre: Esquisse d'une théorie de la pratique, 1972

A Man has a son and a daughter. The daughter is married to father's brother's son (B's son). A's grandson from his son gets married to B's granddaughter from his son and A's daughter:

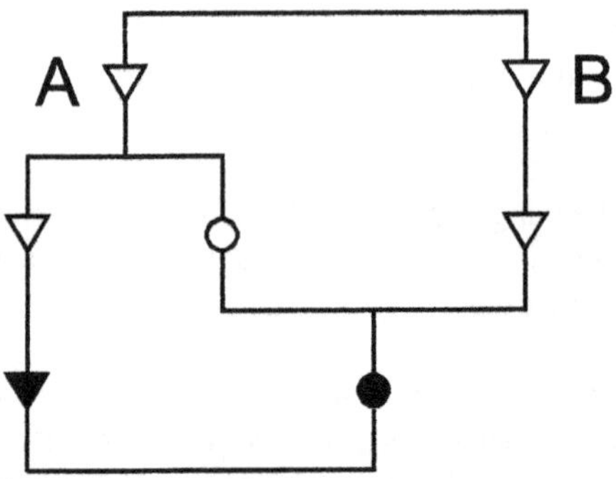

For the groom the bride is his grandfather's brother's granddaughter, for the bride the husband is her mother's brother's son.

Annegret Nippa[127] mentions that when Lévi-Strauss had published "Les structures élementaires de la parenté"[128], those familiar with Arab systems were alarmed not to find the marriage with the patrilateral parallel cousin included in the general investigation, that it took ten years for an explanatory meeting to take place, and that the outcome was by no means explanatory but an exhortation to engage in further studies.

Murphy and Kasdan[129] resume that "the patrilateral parallel cousin marriage is evidently ancient in the Near East, from where it spread during the Arab conquests to adjacent peoples through the vehicles of clientship, intermarriage, and religious conversion". The Arab explanation is reported to be that it keeps property within the family. But this explanation is valid only when the Koranic law, through which a daughter inherits half the amount received by a son, is observed.

---

127 Nippa, Annegret: Haus und Familie in arabischen Ländern, 1991:15

128 Lévi-Strauss, Claude: Les structures élementaires de la parenté, 1949. The respective passage is summarised in: Anthropologie Structurale, 1974:142

129 Murphy, Robert F. and Kasdan, Leonard: The Structure of Parallel Cousin Marriage, 1959:17 bis

As has been pointed out in this study, this argument is not as convincing as some might wish. To hold the family property together could be most easily achieved by not letting women inherit. And if the Koranic law is observed, the daughter from another family might bring additional wealth. But since the special aspect of inheritance is timing and wealth is not inherited at the time of marrying, and may take more than a lifetime to be transferred, the reason cannot be purely materialistic.

Much more convincing is an explanation referring to the structure of society. The parallel cousin marriage was and is preferred since the father's brother's son was, and for those clinging to tradition, still is considered to possess marital rights over his cousin. If he does not take her as a bride, he is expected himself to arrange for another husband and/or consent to his cousin marrying someone else. Musil[130] reports that where there is no patrilateral parallel cousin, the girl falls to the nearest kinsman.

Yemeni women approached on this subject emphasised that this refers predominantly to the past. It is admitted though that elite families still cling to this tradition, not only to keep the family property together but also to remain among themselves. It would also be worth investigating in how far the obligation to provide for family members furnishes a logical argument in favour of father's brother's daughter, or, to return to the other modus of viewing the candidate, mother's brother's son? It was generally pointed out that the poorer the family the fewer the considerations in respect of the genealogy of the marriage partner.

It is also fully appreciated that incest considerations overshadow the bint al-ᶜamm system – but this does not fall within the scope of this study.

4.4 Kinship terminology

A further essential remark in this context must be a reflection on "kinship terminology". Requests for definitions of family relationships are ever and again met with by statements that this or that person is a cousin or a grandson (**ibn al-'ak̲** or **ibn al-bint**). Upon closer investigation the cousin may very well be a grand cousin or even greatgrandcousin, the grandson a greatgrandson, and the grandfather (**jadd**) a fairly remote ancestor. More intriguing still, many young persons claim "grandfatherhood", and this without even being married. It was found that once a

130 Musil, Alois: The manners and customs of the Rwala Bedouins. 1928:137

member of one's generation had children the credit for this achievement was conferred on all other representatives of the generation, too.

But, to return to the above dual modes of approach, as women do not as yet have statistics of their own way of observation, such marriages are still counted as **bint al-ᶜamm** versions. Seen in the context of the Islamic expectation that men provide for women it is not difficult to understand that families try to keep the number of dependent females as small as possible. If a son marries outside his family he has to provide for another female or more of them in addition to his next of kin.

But is this a general concept? Did not the Prophet himself marry a business woman, a rich widow with fabulous wealth of her own? And a woman who managed this wealth on her own? Who only married Mohammad after the latter had proved a good businessman in her employ who could be trusted to look after her affairs?

So maybe there was or is no strict pattern, maybe there has been and is a wide variety of variations, changes and new developments. Both men and women consulted offered a range of opinions and practical examples almost as varied as the number of persons approached.

4.5 Evidence for economic independence of women

A very special mission was undertaken in a further attempt to furnish evidence on how well women are integrated in economic activities in that "bustling city of Sana'a"[131] despite the medieval look and admittedly misleading impression the average traveller, official guest or eager journalist will easily gain and even cherish because this so much appeals to the expectation of a different world. This on the postulation that a genuine feature in the practical life of a woman in Sana'a in the nineties would best be documented by factual testimony of normal practice. If a woman has access to money and is allowed to look after her own affairs, where and how would she do so in modern terms? Presumably at a bank?

131 ᶜAbdulwali, Mohammad Ahmad: ṣanᶜā', madīna maftūḥa, 1986 and Walters, Delores M.: 1987:14

With a personal letter of introduction[132] shown to the vigilant door keepers of banking houses in Sana'a, interviews with the respective bank managers were requested and obtained with no difficulty. In these interviews oral and written confirmation of the number and/or percentage of bank accounts exclusively made out in the name and on behalf of women was requested. The almost enthusiastic reception accorded this request came as a surprise even to the interviewer with her positive attitude towards this line of investigation. Perhaps this is the right place to mention the particular circumstances of a director's office in an Arab city. In accordance with the "Majlis" principle[133] the bank manager will spend several hours a day sitting at his desk and discussing matters with visitors. There is no need to ask for a special appointment. This might seem more convenient to the Western person than it actually is. There will always be many other visitors at the same time, trying to catch the attention of the manager. Any statement made must be phrased so as to be comprehensible to the group since otherwise the speaker will immediately and incessantly be interrupted by the curiosity of fellow visitors. For a researcher it offers a unique opportunity of listening to other people's requests, and of seeing their reaction to one's own. In this particular case the reaction of both the bank managers and the other visitors were genuinely positive.

The banks approached were:

The National Bank of Yemen
The International Bank of Yemen
The United Bank of Yemen
The Arab Bank
The Indosuez Bank
The Kuwait Bank
The Bank for Reconstruction and Development

---

132 This was furnished by Dr. Jussuf Abdullah (who helped in many other ways, too, and proved a most understanding, initiative guide) following a telephone conversation with the head of the Institute of Banking. When the letter was fetched from the Institute the "bearer" was made a most welcome visitor and assured that the type of information requested should have been collected much earlier – if only anyone had thought of doing so ...

133 Dating back to bygone times, the custom of an important person sitting in his **majlis**, or reception room, for several hours every day and being accessible to visitors for sundry requests that may be discussed in public still holds true in daily business life in Sana'a.

There was general agreement that women were perfectly able to run their own affairs and that this should be documented. The procedure for obtaining the data ran to a similar pattern at each bank approached. All the banks do indeed run accounts for women and the relevant employees were instructed to go through the files and establish exact numbers as at the end of 1992. In three cases the right side of the ledger was even shown to the visitor (not the left with the respective amounts, of course) to verify the names were of females. As can be demonstrated by the statements furnished, about 5 % of the bank accounts are in the names of women. In all cases special mention was made of the fact that this was not "fully informative" information since very many couples have joint accounts, i.e. the woman is fully authorised to draw money herself, write out cheques, make dispositions without the prior consent of the husband, but the account is under the name of her husband or even a family account in which several male and female members are involved. Another aspect is the fact that all the accounts exclusively made out in the name of a woman are two-currency accounts, i.e. the women have both rial and dollar deposits. Since the rial is not a convertible currency this indicates that the account holder is versed with dealings abroad, which undoubtedly suggests that these account holders are in all probability representatives of the modern, well educated new generation of women.

4.6 Women's bank accounts – a contradiction in terms?

It must admittedly be seen as the very contradiction of a pattern still widely encountered throughout Sana'a. For the typical Sana'ani woman, and with "typical" the type of informant most commonly encountered on an every-day basis is meant, the man always was, is and should remain "the provider". With only occasional exceptions every woman interviewed claimed that the man provided for the household and all the members of the family living under his roof. And this not on a general basis or in terms of essential purchases but on a day-to-day basis. Many of the women questioned on this subject readily admitted being given household money on a daily basis, or in short intervals. They usually list the items they need, and expect the husband to calculate the appropriate amount required therefor. They never think of returning a single penny and the man is expected to know that. The idea of keeping for another occasion a sum which may still be left, appears a very strange idea indeed. And this attitude is also voiced by modern women and by students who have been abroad and yet have little understanding for the "independent" Western woman in this respect. It might also in some way explain why women with an income of their own feel perfectly justified in keeping all their own money whilst still living at the husband's expense. It certainly helps the

Western mind to understand why Yemeni husbands will sometimes unjustly be reproached for being stingy or not at all generous. They must be fully aware that money given to the woman will be spent to the last coin, if not for the necessary, then for any product that might attract the woman's eye.

And the fact that the new family law of 1992[134] does not incorporate some of the progressive stipulations and formulations to be found in the family law of the former South Yemen on "equal obligations" (Art. 2)[135] exasperates Western representatives of development institutions[136] and promotional bodies, but does not appear to upset the informants approached on this item.

4.7 Interview environment

It is against this multi-faceted background that specific interviews were arranged to collect information on women's inheritance in Sana'a. In order to furnish more items as to the environment encountered and the strategy adopted, a very individual presentation is given of the circumstances that eventually led to the personal interviews undertaken. Be it permitted to refer here to the personal upbringing and experience of the interviewer and of one of her most valuable informants. This in an attempt towards creating more understanding for other ways of behaviour by reciting details pieced together in order to provide the reader with an illustration of at first sight ordinarily amusing incidents devoid all scientific significance or factual evidence for research purposes but which could – it is hoped – initiate a readjustment of established blueprints.

****

Shortly after World War Two had started, Christmas could still be celebrated comfortably in many Central European families. Presents could still be selected according to fashion and personal ideas. One small girl discovered a negro doll under the Christmas tree; the doll was naked, covered with but a flimsy straw skirt. The girl had very much wanted the doll and went on searching under the Christmas tree for the doll's outfit. It was winter, the weather was icy cold, the new doll needed clothes. The girl could not imagine that Santa Claus in all his wisdom and

---

134 **al-jarīda al-rasmiya** 3, **qānūn aḥwāl aš-šaksiya** 20/1992

135 **qānūn al-usra** 1/1974 (DPRY)

136 Johnson, Catherine, in the 1992 Contribution on Women's Legal Rights, ICD Publication

generosity should have forgotten to bring clothes and said so aloud. An indignant grandmother advised her that the new doll, called "Samba", had come from a tropical country where it was warm and so did not need any clothes. The girl pointed out that this might well be, but that Europe was another matter, and being here Samba would catch cold without clothes. The girl suggested a compromise, she would give half of her European doll's clothes to the new doll. This was strictly opposed by the family. Samba was a negro, he could not possibly be given a white doll's clothes. The girl was in despair. She was overwhelmed by a suspicion that not only was Santa Claus not so very wise but that there was something wrong in the attitudes of the grown-ups she lived with – and that she ought to try to find ways and means to make them understand ...

*****

In a remote little village up in the mountains outside Taiz in Yemen, when this country was still ruled by the Imam, a girl was born into a respectable, tradition-bound family and was brought up as befitted the people around her – without electricity or indoor water. She had never seen a telephone, had never moved outside her village. Then one day she was told that her future husband, the son of her father's brother, whom she recalled from playing together when both had been children, would arrive from the United States, where he had graduated, to marry her. The wedding was celebrated with much ado, the husband had to leave after only a few days to take up a teaching post at an American University. The young wife was delivered of a daughter, and when the child was three years old the husband ordered his wife and the child to join him in the United States. She was driven to Taiz by a member of the family, was put onto a plane to Cairo where she was told she would have to find her plane to the U.S. She could speak and read Arabic only, but had been given a piece of paper with her husband's address and her flight number on it. She managed to catch her plane to Washington, clutching an equally frightened daughter to her bosom for a little bit of warmth and comfort:

"I was frightfully hungry and when the stewardess put a strange looking tray in front of me, I snatched the whole piece of meat from it, gnawed at it and took small chunks off it to put them into my daughter's mouth – for survival. As time went on I became ever more frightened. What strange world was this, where the sun would never set? I had left home in the morning and after so many hours I arrived on this very same morning? And whenever I ventured to look around me through my veil I was appalled by the sight of men and women embracing and kissing at the airport in public, the women nearly naked. My husband drove me and the child to an immense house, where hundreds of people had apartments. I was ushered into one with most unfamiliar objects, so many high tables and chairs, cupboards and closets and beds on poles and what they called "bathrooms", where I was told to sit on a huge white oval bowl. To make life easier for me, my husband had suggested taking us to a restaurant for meals so that I could slowly arrange my own household, but he was discouraged after the first try. I had done my best to imitate the persons around me who skillfully used metal instruments for eating, and seemed to enjoy sitting on chairs at tables. I could not cope with all this and did not know what to tell my daughter. The "wonderful T-bone steak" my husband insisted I would love, slipped to the floor every time I tried to cut off a bite. I had overlooked having to pin it down with the fork while 'working' at it ... I was made fun off, ridiculed and a disgrace to my husband. I had to do better. And as quickly as at all possible."

She had decided she would manage. She simply had to survive, for her own sake and that of her child. And she managed extremely well, while remaining a genuine Yemeni woman and remaining proud of it.

*****

It was an afternoon about 50 years after World War Two when the two women, by that time both grandmothers, sat together on the cushioned floor of a **mafraj**[137] in an old house in Sana'a. They had met by pure coincidence and had become close friends at first sight. They had agreed to meet an hour before all the other ladies invited to the qat-chewing party were expected to show up, to discuss very private, truly serious matters that were on both their minds, could not be spoken of in the presence of silly, inexperienced, young female relatives, and not even mentioned with men present. But both had been aware that it would be a "gathering in style" and had dressed carefully. The European guest had become accustomed to discovering how exquisitely dressed all the women would be once they had deposited their **sitāra** or **šaršaf**[138] [139] in the entrance hall. She for herself, to please her hostess, had made sure to put on "the latest in Paris fashion" under the cloak she always wore out of doors out of respect for Sana'ani tradition. When the lady

---

137 The room to receive and entertain guests. In houses of well-to-do families, two such rooms will be provided so that men and women may entertain simultaneously, but separately. Where only one room is available, parties must be organised on different days.

138 The traditional outdoor covers as worn by women in Sana'a

139 For a more detailed explanation of outdoor covers as worn by Yemeni women, see Mundy in R. Lewcock and R.B. Serjeant, 1983:Chapter 25 (Women's Dresses:535-538)

of the house spotted a unique little Biedermeier bracelet on the European woman's arm, she clucked with delight.

"Did your husband give this to you when you married?"

"No, I inherited it from my grandmother. I had always admired it and asked her to bequeath it to me in her will."

There was a long moment of silence. The silence during which Europeans say an angel passes through the room and which Muslims ascribe to a second of eternity during which Allah inspires men to enlightened thinking. The European woman realised that she had referred to a custom for which she would find it difficult to quote an opposite in Islamic society; the Arab woman's eyes widened for a very short spell, in what can only be interpreted as wishful thinking, before she blinked and her eyes narrowed again and her guest knew she had found an explanation why Allah in his wisdom had provided in this case another acquisition procedure for his believers.

"Do you know how we 'inherit'?"

"Isn't this specified in the holy Koran? ..."

"And the Sharia, and the constitution, and tribal law, and?"

"?"

"... it is the easiest thing to understand. Use your common sense. Forget your academic education. Think of the innate wisdom of us women!"

"Will you help me to find out?"

"Allah will help you."

*****

4.8 The interviews

From the many interviews held and sessions recorded only the most suitable are presented. It should also be pointed out that drafts of the written record for each interview actually used were made at once and discussed with the women concerned before they were finally incorporated. With very few exceptions, more than one woman had been present at each interview, as all the women always seemed to be much more at ease when in company and as it was considered helpful to let the interviewer have more persons available to draw information from. Not only were all the women very outspoken and ready to give any further explanation that might be wanted, the accuracy in the replies of the "main" person interviewed was very often confirmed by others present, emphasising that this or that had indeed been so in her particular case while what a neighbour or cousin also present had experienced had been altogether different.

It should perhaps be mentioned that the selection was made according to specific items cropping up in individual interviews. While each of the interviews undertaken rendered valuable information in general terms, some proved especially helpful in furnishing answers to the practical aspect of inheritance rules encountered in texts. It should perhaps also be disclosed that the interviewer in some instances met with such unexpected confirmation of a theory discussed in books that a considerable amount of effort was required not to show this and remain matter-of-fact and to cross check twice before taking the notes back home.

The only exclusively one-woman interviews are those with Samira and Aisha, both representing very modern women, one partly educated abroad, one practically living in two worlds. As the number of such females is expected to increase rapidly, they are considered to represent a feature of Sana'a today becoming increasingly typical. It is also obvious that they exert an enormous influence on their neighbours and friends and are constantly approached for advice and opinion.

4.8.1 Samira: **a sāda**

a representative of the very modern women, an example of division of inheritance without any documents

Samira is chosen to start the part of the study dealing with reality as encountered in Yemen today, not so much because she is a representative of the **sāda**, but because she proved to be an infinitely valuable source of information and elucidation that will help towards better understanding of the statements made in subsequent interviews. Because of her long stays in the United States and her familiarity with other cultures and concepts she even phrases her sentences in a way that fits into Western lines of thought, and can point out the subtleties she wants to have conveyed. She is also a unique example of a modern women, accustomed to moving in academic circles, skillfully performing a demanding job while clinging to Islamic and Yemeni traditions out of conviction and a natural affinity, a devoted mother persuading her children to accept the necessity of securing one's place in both worlds and making them work towards this end. She is immensely anxious to live a Yemeni life in Sana'a, in order not to offend any member of her family or neighbour, but she makes sure she remains her individual self. Graceful movements are made even more exquisite by her taste in becoming dresses, and no cloak or veil can hide the choreographically designed way she walks. Huge black eyes look at you when she converses, full of candour and delight.

Samira's father was a diplomat of the old style, that is to say of aristocratic origin, serving his country the way his rank and personal abilities permitted, and also because he could afford to, and not with a view to making money out of a "job". Samira's mother was his fourth wife, in whom he had become interested when the ladies of the two families had mentioned and referred to her in their function of discussing and arranging marriages. She was 13 when she was married to a man 20 years her senior. She became pregnant at the onset of puberty and was delivered of a healthy child. When this child died in an accident before the mother's eyes she suffered such a severe shock that she left Sana'a and stayed in a village for one year to recover. Her husband agreed to this since he had other wives to be with during her absence. It took seven years for her to bear another healthy child, Samira, and her husband agreed to leave it at that and not to insist on any further pregnancies. Thus the little girl was an "only" child of her mother, which certainly also explains the very close relationship that was to develop, but had any amount of brothers and sisters from her father with his other wives. When she was three years old, the family moved to the United States in the wake of the 1962 revolution. She attended elementary and secondary school there, but also received all the education she would have been given in Yemen. Her father insisted that all his children study the Koran and supervised them to make sure that they understood the meaning of every verse and did not only learn the text by heart. He discussed every item with his children and made them realise that they would always find guidance and explanation for every question that might crop up in their lives – but that they would have to look for the appropriate verse. The children were always allowed to speak out and ask questions. When Samira was in her "stormy" teens she argued for women's rights, and questioned the unfair concept of four legal wives, and the unfair division of inheritance. She was made to understand the background against which these rules were conceived and that she had to study closely what seemed unfair at first sight. She eventually reached a stage where she was able to accept what she had found and decided to abandon further enquiries "for the time being", but has ever since considered the Koran as her encyclopaedia, and has ever and again turned to it in every phase of her further development.

When she was 18, she was married to a Yemeni of another sāda family temporarily established in the United States. The two families had known each other for many years.

"So it was an arranged marriage?"

"I always feel unhappy about this term: there is a wrong conception in it. It is not true that the principals involved have no control. It is really that the parents should be seen as consultants you engage. It is their natural role. They have more experience, they know more, can guide you. All the information they gather or can gather about the potential partner might never become known to you. They act like a shield and can protect you from a hasty mistake. It is also a step in the process of your development to learn to acknowledge the parents' role, to learn to accept advice before you take such an important step as getting married."

"But you knew the man you would marry?"

"Well, I had met him, I knew who he was and what he did. And when marriage was considered, I discussed things with him. But you see, I was, perhaps, very lucky, I felt it would work with him. There is some chemistry in you that tells you. And there was a lot of agreement between the two of us at first sight. Still, I much preferred having my father and my mother act on my behalf in their respective fields. There are very delicate matters in a marriage which you can hardly expect a young girl to lay down for herself. In my case it was agreed that I would not have children immediately, but would finish my studies and have a profession. And that even if I had children I would always finish my studies and work."

"Forgive me for interrupting you, but I find it difficult to imagine the drafting of a marriage contract stating that you are not ready to have children while you are supposed to consummate the marriage to make it valid?"

"And that is exactly because you Westerners have a wrong concept of a marriage contract: A marriage contract should be an arrangement for practical purposes. If consummation of the marriage is desired and the woman is not to become pregnant, the husband must be obliged to control himself, to take care and withdraw before ejaculation. If he cannot do this he must agree to contraception. This is a question of family honour. The West has as yet to grasp what family honour means in Islam. On the basis of a marriage contract to this effect the young wife can refuse to have sexual intercourse if the husband does not abide by the rules. It is the honour of both families which is at stake. But you will understand that it is much better for such a contract to be drawn up by the parents and not the marriage partners themselves."

"And what was arranged in terms of **mahr** in your case?"

"Oh, I know that this has become a subject of endless discussion in social anthropology – because it is a topic for which almost every family or category of families has an individual solution. With us the husband gives certain values to the bride when he marries. He is, of course, also responsible for all the costs of the home and the household. The woman can do as she likes with her money or valuable things. It is only when she wants a divorce that she would have to pay back the mahr."

"Thus you would say a woman under such circumstances would be wise to keep her mahr intact?"

"That may very well be so. But then, everything is negotiable, she might get the money for a divorce from her family if they agree to the idea, or the husband might waive his claim."

"And if your mahr is still with you when you grow old, can you leave it to a certain person?"

"Theoretically yes, you could write a will. But this would mean that relations with your family are very bad indeed, that there is no trust between the members of your family. It is assumed that everyone tacitly accepts that jewelry should be passed on to a woman's daughters. Only if a mother fears there might be dispute would she give things to her daughters before her death. If you feel there is harmony in your life, no will making is necessary. Parents should know their children, they may want to protect one of them, or make sure there will be fair play. My father-in-law is a man given to second thoughts and suspicion, he updates his will once a year."

"And your mother and father?"

"My mother had had an inheritance from her father but did not want her brothers to discuss shares with me as the only daughter. Thus when I got married she made over all her money to me directly to look after it, I mean she did not go via documents. As a Muslim you make your decisions with Allah. The relationship between the two of us was such that she was sure I would always look after her and do my best for her. But I was afraid that if I passed away before my mother, my husband and my children would inherit my mother's money from me and she would not get a share, so I told my father that I would want this money to go back to my mother who, we all knew, would always look after my husband and her grandchildren."

"And when your mother died?"

"My father duly inherited much money since my mother had no sons. But he never claimed it and even made over this money to me. But as he would be a beneficiary upon my death I could not give away his portion of my mother's money without previously asking for his consent."

"So you do not recall any dispute or intrigue. The famous Yemeni proverb "la tuarrith ibnak ya'adak"[140] (Do not pass on your wealth to your children while you live) does not apply in your family?"

"For my family honesty is a question of personal honour. Money for us is not as important as honour. We have been offered money for many things but did not want such money, we have been offered positions we did not want to assume. We try to pass this on to our children. But I fully realise that we can very well be satisfied with what we have and share this without anyone going wanting. There are other things at stake for us than money ..."

Samira went out to tell the children that they should get ready to accompany her to a social gathering. Her youngest daughter rushed in to show the interviewer a particularly sticky piece of coloured bubble gum. Her eyes beamed with delight:

"Look what I was given by my elder sister! She bought it specially for me."

"Could you not have bought it with your own pocket money?"

---

140 Goitein, S.D.F.: Jemenica, Sprichwörter und Redensarten aus Zentral-Jemen, 1970: No. 999

"No I am only six, I am too small to have money of my own, they say I do not know what money is worth and how to use it properly. I must always ask for everything."

Walking down the unevenly shaped spiral staircase of one of the oldest houses in Sana'a it was as if centuries of tradition oozed from the crevices in the stone walls. The sound of the heavy wooden door swinging back on its hinges to close with a thump, finished an episode of insight into ancient times made understandable, graspable, fathomable.

4.8.2 Aisha: a career woman and a devoted mother an example of land given to a female within the family while the rights to this land were retained

Aisha agreed to a detailed interview if the questions could be asked while she was on duty at the National Institute for Personnel Administration but would not be too busy with work. She also made sure that it was understood that the interviewer would, of course, be invited to her house for a meal, or even several, but that, as there were children in the house who were accustomed to having access to their mother and to guests during the little time that was left of a day spent apart, it was self-evident that it would be impossible to concentrate on such serious work as the interview at home.

The first two sessions were not very successful as far as the interview itself was concerned, as the office was literally stormed by other members of the institute. Aisha shared the suspicion of the interviewer that many of the requests for immediate attention could not be attributed to the urgency of the matter but were due to curiosity to see the guest. They did give the guest a fair amount of insight into the working habits, though, and this in particular as regards the relationship between a female senior and male juniors.

On the third day the situation took a most favourable turn. Aisha decided not to attend a staff meeting in which a resolution for better working conditions was to be drafted, but delegated all the other members of her department to this meeting. The call for mid-day prayer was the first sign of ongoing activities outside the office.

Aisha is a delicately shaped women of 35, with very graceful movements and an immensely becoming smile that seems to remain in her eyes even when she veils the lower part of her face. Her eyes speak a language that carries information even before her mouth forms the words.

She was born in Taiz as the third child of a merchant family, stemming from a village near the town. Her father had taken up a government job and moved to Taiz after marrying her mother when he was 25 and the bride 16. The two families had been neighbours in the village and the marriage had been arranged by the mothers. Aisha has six brothers and two sisters. At the age of six she went to an elementary school for girls, followed by three years of preparatory school and three further years of secondary school in Taiz. She then studied at Sana'a University for four years and obtained her bachelor's degree at the Faculty of Arts. During her studies in Sana'a she stayed at the house of her uncle and visited her family in Taiz regularly. During one of these visits, when she had just turned 17, she met her father's sister's son who at that time had been studying engineering in Russia and was on a visit back home too. The two agreed to get married after termination of their studies. They had both spent a full summer vacation back home and had met on several occasions when the extended family assembled. They had subsequently also been permitted to see each other and discuss their marriage without anyone else being present.

Aisha obtained a scholarship in the United States of America and got her MA there. She returned to Yemen and got married when she was 27. By that time her husband had become a government employee, and she had started a career at the National Institute. The couple so far have a daughter of six and a boy of two. Aisha never interrupted her work – except for the 40 days a woman is required to stay in her house after having given birth to a child. For the delivery of both of her children she had returned to her parents' house in Taiz and had altogether spent about two months there on both occasions.

Aisha adores her children and could not imagine a life without them. On the other hand she is devoted to her profession and does not go to work merely for the sake of earning money. She is fully aware of the conflict between genuine love for her professional activities and her responsibilities and priorities as a mother. While doing her best to make up for any loss in care and attention as a result of professional obligations and interests, she tries not to spoil the children to "make up for a bad conscience", but very often finds herself thinking twice before scolding them. She feels convinced, though, that she would not be as patient and accommodating with her children if she had them with her all day, but she makes sure the weekend is spent together with them, and only invites guests who appreciate this. She only had a maid for as long as it was absolutely necessary before the children could be enrolled in kindergarten.

The family lives in a small rented house, with a traditional **ḥammām**[141] and a (for Western standards) very moderately furnished kitchen. A huge TV set including a video recorder in the living room is considered a matter of course as is a PC in the parent's bedroom/study. There are two cars in the family but it is explicitly pointed out that the husband has an official car because of his job with the government, and the wife needs a means of individual transportation.

"Do you remember when you gave a thought to 'inheritance' because of a personal matter?"

"Oh, yes, it was only a few months ago, when we bought the plot of land to have our house constructed on."

"Our house?"

"Well, since both of us are working, each paid half of the sum required and this was written down in the purchase contract, so that if my husband dies before me, I can furnish proof that only half of the house belongs to him."

"Would it not suffice for your husband to leave a will?"

"According to the Koran, a will can be made to the amount of one third of a man's property only, and as a good Muslim he must not make a will that would hurt the ones he leaves behind. If he owned the whole house, he could not make it over to me in full without curtailing the children's shares, not to speak of other members of our family entitled to obligatory shares."

"But then you would not get the other half once he dies."

"It will be my house by that time, inshallah. I will be buying the other half out of my salary in regular instalments. But anyway, my situation has greatly improved with the birth of my son. You see, a son is like a wall, he protects his sisters from uncles who would otherwise inherit. Our family has a very good relationship, we have a tradition of keeping the parents' house for all the family. When my father died, my

---

141 Usually one tiled or oil-painted room with a shower and a toilet consisting of a hole in the floor and two foot props or a china basin with a bottom outlet and corrugated side boards to put one's feet on. Flushing is either accomplished manually from a water jug or there is a water tap with a hose on it or, in the more modern version, a reservoir proper with a chain to pull.

mother kept the house, and my brothers and sisters share the cost of maintaining it for her. We only had the Qadi write down the appropriate shares in case the house had to be sold one day, so that everyone would get what was due. But we had to be careful about my father's father who would have inherited from my mother upon her death. This is why my father had made over the house to her in return for the contributions she had always made to the running of the household from the payments she had received from her brothers on an annual basis since she had not insisted on receiving her share of the land when her father died but had left her share to them to look after."

"And all your brothers look after the land together?"

"No, none of them, the land was leased to a stranger, we only receive and share the money accruing. There was also a piece of land in town, this was sold to a construction company to build apartments on. One of my brothers retained the right to manage these apartments and let them. Very shortly after that he had an accident and died. He left a wife and two sons. His managing rights were entrusted to another brother until the children were of age. Still, the family would have been badly off, had not my grandfather, who was a very rich man, made a will that the money due to my brother would be for his children if my brother died before him. But let me point out again, our main concern is always to keep the family property in our hands. A right to inherit is regarded and treated as an own income. And girls sometimes do not insist on getting their shares in order to ensure better relations and a better standing in the family. And this can very well also happen with men. My husband inherited a piece of land and registered it under his name, but gave it to his sister to build a house on it, which again will be registered under my husband's name. This was done to avoid the property possibly passing into the hands of my husband's sister's husband, who is not from our family. This is done for protection and not out of disregard for the woman."

"So you actually bought land for a house of your own while a plot available from your husband's side was not used and was given to your husband's sister instead?"

"This is due to two reasons. We wanted a house in a particular area of Sana'a where there are many trees to make sure our children will grow up in a healthy environment. The plot of land I told you about is in Taiz which is convenient for my husband's sister, and, anyway, since we are of the same family, it still belongs to us. You see, if for some reason my parents' house in Taiz was no longer available or convenient I could always go to my husband's sister's house."

"And you actually receive money from property you did not insist on inheriting shares of?"

"In my case I do not, since it concerns a house the family lives in. But the right to my room in the house is vouchsafed by my not insisting on receiving money. This money is my contribution to the upkeep of the house."

"And if you had inherited shares in land?"

"Well, land is never passed on to a minor nor at the time of marriage. For a minor it is entrusted to a custodian, with a woman her share is suspended until later so that her son will get the land, especially if it is all one family, so that nothing gets lost or is taken away by a division."

"Thus land is not **mahr** or part of it?"

"Not as far as I could imagine. In my family **mahr** will only be transferred to a woman upon divorce. If the woman dies the husband can keep the **mahr** he agreed to pay to her in the marriage contract."

"And if the husband dies before the wife, then what happens to her **mahr**?"

"It goes to all those inheriting in accordance with the rules of the Koran. But I know that other families do it differently. You must remember we are from Taiz. However, so many originally from Taiz live in Sana'a now, so you will encounter this particular way of handling inheritance in other families, too."

"So you would agree to defining that you inherit according to the Koran, but that your **mahr** arrangements are "**ᶜurf**?"

"If you agree to see this as not conflicting with our holy Koran, I might be prepared to see it like this, yes."

"Would you mind my asking you whether you are familiar with all the inheritance rules, I mean, what your legal rights are or would be?"

"No, I don't mind at all. You have come to see me to ask questions. But as I said, it is all in the Koran. The details are explained in the Sharia, and the laws in force in Yemen are based on the Sharia. I do not know everything in detail. I can rely on the Qadi we have in our family, who is called upon when the situation arises. But we have, as far as I can remember, never litigated over inheritance. We trust our husbands, fathers and brothers to divide justly. I mean, if my husband cannot be trusted to look after my interests in an inheritance question, what could a court do for me?"

"And one more consideration: since it is impossible to by-pass Koranic inheritance shares and wills are only possible up to one third of one's property, could not a father make a gift to a beloved child he might want to get more from him?"

"This is not very practical – I mean, if it concerns a bigger share. First of all, the father would not know for how long he is going to live, he might need the share himself. Secondly, if he makes over a huge share and dies immediately afterwards this would not be considered the behaviour of a good Muslim."

"So you are content with the inheritance rules? You would not want a change in the law, not even in respect to the half share of a woman?"

"Not as long as the man is the legal provider. You know, I could keep my salary to myself ..."

"You don't?"

"Well, I do not contribute to the household as such. My husband would feel offended if he thought he was not able to provide for the family. But I contribute extras that would not be necessary, but which all the family like and enjoy."

"And your husband is happy with this arrangement?"

"Oh yes, perfectly so. Of course, I discuss everything with him. You must understand, he likes the idea that he provides all the necessaries and essentials and I contribute extras that would not be really needed ...

4.8.3 Malika: a very young wife, still at school, she fully trusts the men in her family, but her in-laws furnish examples for women cheated out of **mahr**

- women cheated out of inheritance
- women realising unfair division and going to court

Malika is the only woman met via her husband, that is to say the husband asked the interviewer to consider his wife as an informant. She was originally contacted on the principle of never turning down an informant suggested by a person who had proved to be a helpful contact.

Malika is only 18 and the youngest of all the married women interviewed. A relatively light-skinned, astonishingly tall woman for Yemeni standards, very shy, and visibly not quite at ease with foreigners. She on her side had only consented to the interview because her husband had suggested that her information "might help other women".

Her family and that of her husband had lived in the same village, the two mothers are sisters. Both families moved to Sana'a several years ago when the two fathers transferred their merchant business to the capital. Malika had always known her mother's sister's son who had always been considered a particularly bright boy. She also found him good-looking, of gentle temper, and immensely well educated. He had already obtained a master's degree and was writing his thesis for a Ph.D. when the parents suggested marriage. Malika was only too pleased to accept, the more so as she was assured that she could finish her training to become a teacher and that her future husband would agree to her taking a job. The money he paid as **mahr** and **šarṭ** had come from his father and was paid to her father who still keeps her **mahr** for her, the **šarṭ** was spent on furnishing a small flat with a minimum of household utensils – with a gas **tannur**[142] as the object of special pride. Malika had her first child, a daughter, within nine months of her wedding, and continues to go to school. The baby is looked after by her mother while she studies, but she runs her own household with the help and practical assistance of her husband. The interview took place in the afternoon, when the baby was asleep.

"Do you like life in Sana'a or would you prefer to live in the country where you were born?"

"I still miss my village very much. But I could not have gone to my school and would not become a teacher, and this means very much to me. But I would not like to stay here without my mother living just around the corner. And I do miss my sister and my brothers who are much older and have their families out there. The best times are those when we go back to our village for the weekend together."

"But you enjoy having this small flat of your own – with only your husband and the baby?"

---

142 = the special oven to make **malūj**, the thin crisp bread

"As long as I have my mother near by I find it very agreeable, yes."

"Did you want to have a baby so soon?"

"We left this to Allah and he blessed us with a child. And all my family is very happy, my husband is the proudest of all. And as I am permitted to go to school I think it is alright."

"Your husband seems to help you a lot?"

"He adores his daughter and feels disadvantaged that only I can feed her. But he changes her nappies and talks to her a lot. He also does all the shopping whenever possible so that I only have to go out and buy the things he is not familiar with."

"So how are your financial arrangements? Do you have money of your own?"

"No, I don't need to. I ask my husband for money whenever I need it. I tell him all the articles I want and he calculates what this will cost."

"And if something is more or less expensive?"

"???? – I look for the things I want for the price I can pay, or I bargain for them."

"And you never want to buy anything without your husband knowing about it? If you want to buy a present for him, you tell him beforehand?"

"Oh, no. You see, my husband does not have such a good memory for these things. He does not always keep track of what I already bought last week. So if I need money for something special I tell him I need something I already have."

"And if he one day tells you he has no money?"

"Then I must wait and pray to Allah to help us."

"What about your **mahr**?"

"My father keeps it for me as a security. I don't think I would have to ask for it. If we really came to be hard up, my father would help us anyway."

"And if your father passes away?"

"My brothers are good Muslims, they would either give me my share if something was sold upon my father's death or, if our land is kept, make contributions to me from my share which they would keep and look after for me."

"But you would then want your **mahr**?"

"Not really, I would rather keep it there and pass it on to the next generation, I mean, to my children. You never know what the times might bring for them. And as long as my husband looks after me, I want to save it for other times."

"And what would you do if – contrary to all expectations and to the very good relations within your family you discovered one day that you were not receiving fair treatment, if you no longer received contributions?"

"If this meant my children went hungry I would go to court, but only then. You see, I have all the papers about what and how much belongs to me. But this would be the end of our family."

At that moment Malika's mother came into the room, a very resolute woman who immediately insisted that we all "eat" instead of merely "discussing". She had brought two neighbours and a basket with sweets. Malika's mother could only be described in baroque terms: despite the loose gown a considerable amount of body was discernable; sitting cross-legged on the floor she seemed to roll over to one side or the other at every movement, while nothing escaped her attention. Without waiting for any introduction or question she burst out:

"You understand nothing about inheritance. You are not a Muslim, you are absolutely ignorant. You annoy Allah with all your concepts and ideas of independence. What do you want to be independent from?"

She was assured that the interviewer was trying very hard in all she did not to annoy Allah and that the visit was paid primarily to congratulate her on her fine daughter and to thank Allah for his grace in having blessed her with a child, and also to tell her how well her son-in-law was progressing at university and how pleased she could be with her family. This met with the unanimous approval of the two accompanying ladies. One was very old and skinny, hollow-cheeked, visibly worn out by hard labour and lack of care, her back bent, her hands and feet full of scars and burns. The other one was a replica of a French concierge, who had entered the room knitting and never stopped, as she also never stopped dropping grumbled remarks. From her looks it was obvious that she knew everyone and everything and that nothing would be new or surprising for her.

"As you can see", Malika's mother resumed the conversation, "we are a very happy family. I knew what I agreed to when I married my husband. He knew what he was in for. He always provides me with the money I need. But I know how to spend it. I do not need a lawyer to tell me. When my father died, I was wise not to insist on my share of the land. Can you see me ploughing the fields myself? My brothers do that for me. And whenever I was in childbed they sent all the food my family needed for a full two weeks, and at every **ʿaīd**[143] I get new clothes. And my unclaimed share is a sure means of avoiding dispute. Whenever my brothers quarrel for more than five minutes I enter their room and threaten that I would withdraw my share if they do not settle amicably."

"But if you were absent one of these days or your brothers decided to sell the land, now that prices have gone up so much?"

"I can rely on my brothers. If they sell, I would get the money for my share. They could not sell without our neighbours knowing of this. So, even if they tried to cheat me, I would be told in good time."

"And you would take steps?"

"Take steps? I would go to the Qadi before sunset. He is from our village, he knows me and knows what to do."

The black skinny woman only sighed. But Malika's mother snatched her from her mattress and positioned her in front of the interviewer:

"She is a monstrous case. She has a tale I can hardly believe myself."

Zeinab was born in a village just outside Sana'a, she had four sisters and five brothers. Her father died when she was ten. Her brother acted as her guardian. The estate was not divided, the brothers had decided to postpone this, the sisters were content to be able to stay on in the house and be looked after (fed). Her brother then found a husband for her who gave silver as mahr to the brother, who with it bought a cow for his own farm. Zeinab was so ashamed, and refused to admit that

143 = the traditional feast at the end of Ramadan

her brother could be such a bad person, that she said nothing and followed her new husband to the house of her mother-in-law. She was a most welcome servant for her, did all the menial jobs, and had to wear what was given to her. She never had a single rial to herself since the mother-in-law ran the household and her son was a coward, never daring to contradict his mother.

Ten years after she had got married, she learned that her brothers had finally divided her father's estate in the absence of the sisters, retaining the latters' shares for themselves. She asked to be allowed to visit her old home and went to the Sheikh to ask for his help and intervention. The Sheikh summoned the brothers. When the brothers returned from the Sheikh they threatened Zeinab saying she would never be able to go to her father's house again if she insisted on her share, no one in the village would communicate with her. If she kept silent, though, they would visit her and bring her a sheep every year. She could not resist the temptation of having her new neighbours see that. Ever since once a year she has led the sheep through the street she lives in before it is slaughtered and then could and can invite all the neighbours and be generous.

"You see, it is not so bad now. My mother-in-law finally died. Since then I have had no problems with my husband, he even buys a little bit of Qat for me now and again in addition to the money I can ask him for now I run the household. It is very little though. I have never done any shopping myself, I prefer to let him do this as he always did. And I was told I would get a pension should he die before me."

"But you do not have children to stay with, would you then live by yourself?"

"No, certainly not, I would go back home, to my brothers. If I give them the pension money, I will be doubly welcome ..."

The "concierge" had had enough. She gathered her belongings and informed the other women that there was a women's party going on around the corner and she would hate to miss more of the gossip that must have been going on there. Surely only ordinary gossip but you never know when you might miss an important detail. It was not long after she had departed that Malika's mother-in-law slipped in. She apologised for not having welcomed the guest earlier on but explained she had wanted to make sure the head informant of the whole street (the knitter) was gone before she was prepared to add to the information on female inheritance she had been told was being requested.

It turned out that for a practical understanding of Malika's mother-in-law's family a chart was the only solution:

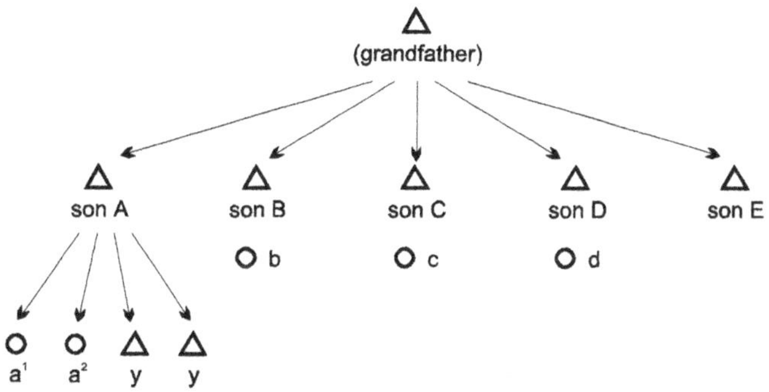

The mother-in-law's grandfather had died and left 5 sons. Upon an oral agreement no division of inheritance was made. Sons A, B, C and D died before a division was made. Son A had left two daughters and two sons (a^1 = Malika's mother-in-law). Sons B, C, and D had left one daughter each (b,c,d), Son E is still alive and has sons and daughters but these do not count as long as he is there.

The division was made twenty years ago, in the absence of all of the females concerned. The legacy consisted of land and houses. Malika's mother-in-law would have been entitled to more since her brothers had died without male children, so that she should have received her **radd** portion. When she discovered this she and two of her female cousins (b and d) sent d's husband as their representative to the Court to protest against the division made in 1974 and to initiate proceedings for the sale of land to be revoked. The Court accepted the case, but it was pointed out that the proceedings would take a long time since many sides were affected. If the division were revoked this would mean that those who bought the land would have to renegotiate the terms.

"So you did not check on how much you got when the division was made?"

"No, I absolutely trusted my brothers and my father's brother."

"And when you found out – how did you and why didn't you try to come to an amicable arrangement with your brothers?"

"I probably would never have noticed. It was my father's brother who one day wanted to take out a loan on his share of the land and also wanted to sell part of it.

He wanted me to consent to sell part of my share too and lend him the money so that he could start a bigger business. It was the first time I saw the papers and started reviewing them. I was very, very upset. An amicable settlement had become altogether impossible, part of my land had been sold twenty years ago ..."

4.8.4 Munira: cuddled wife of a university professor, not interested in studying, but extremely well informed on division of inheritance, example of a **kalāla** and of a contested **waṣīya**

Munira insisted on pouring the tea herself. Beautifully dressed and wearing a whole collection of jewelry she was comfortably resting against the partition cushions on the mafraj mattresses, all in scarlet velvet. The room was full of heavy perfumes, hostess and guests multiplied in an ingenious arrangement of mirrors. The tea had been brought in with heaps and piles of sweets in various colours by an unobtrusive Indian maid. It was a modern house, looking brand-new but built in line with Sana'ani tradition, in stone and wood, and with coloured **qamarīya**[144] windows. It had a Western-style bathroom, a separate[145] bedroom imported from Italy, the kitchen housed a **tannur** and a microwave oven. It had taken quite some time to admire all the details of the spacious house. It was also obvious that someone must be travelling a lot and gathering souvenirs of all kinds and from all parts of the world.

"In such beautiful surroundings you surely like to be at home?"

"Oh yes, very much so, it is my realm, I think twice before going out. My husband brings everything I need or think of – and many things that I do not know at all what their use is."

"And before you got married, you never wanted to see the world?"

"Not without a special purpose. I found it boring enough to go to school every day, I absolutely refused to go to University. I got married when I was 18. My husband was 47 at that time. Our two families have always been **guḍā'**, there are so many wise men around that I can attend to what I like doing and need not bother my head

---

144 = the upper, semi-circular part of a window

145 A separate bedroom is still a rare achievement. It is considered a waste of space. People prefer to sleep in a room they use for many other activities too. Very often a mattress is rolled out in the evening and stored away during the day.

about what will become of me. If my husband very much wants me to I accompany him on his academic visits to other universities, but this is usually no fun at all. And since our son is at a private school abroad I sometimes have to go there on my own to visit him when my husband is otherwise engaged."

"And you run this huge house and have guests almost every afternoon. Do you never run out of food or other essential items while your husband is away?"

"Then I send the maid or our chauffeur shopping."

"So you have money of your own?"

"There is money in my husband's writing desk and I take out as much as I need. I also have an account of my own at the bank, but I do not use it. You see, I get interest on shares in a company and this money is deposited at the bank."

"Have you made a will to make sure it will go to your son one day?"

"No, I am against writing wills. You should not make any decision before Allah decides about you. He might feel you were interfering with his dispositions."

"So you are leaving everything to be arranged according to the Koran and do not intend to make provisions in view of the many males in your family?"

"Well, I should perhaps tell you that we have a way of our own in my family. There is, as you know, always the possibility to waive a claim to inheritance in favour of another member of the family. And also, our grandfathers have made **awqāf** for the benefit of family members not getting huge shares to recompense them. No one is in need. So far this system has supported us very well, but with our present generation going abroad so much and spending money, huge sums of money, on ridiculous things, I am not happy. Until now we always considered it just and reasonable to spread the family's wealth evenly, and there was enough so that everyone could be content. But times have changed. Individual members of the family are making exorbitant demands. I do not want to see the day they start arguing."

And almost inaudibly she whispered: "I really pray a lot that Allah may show them what is to be done. But it is not considered appropriate for a good Muslim to worry. It is certainly also because I have seen what happens when a family starts questioning the division of an inheritance. I have heard my father and his brothers - **all guḍā'** - discuss cases - it always reminds me of one proverb: 'ma ktar as-si? gal gassimoh'[146] (How much is this? You try and divide it! – If great fortunes are divided in the course of inheritance processes, there is usually not much left)."

"But if someone really feels he or she has been cheated, what else should you do but appeal to a court?"

"That is exactly what I am so much concerned about. I do realise I am in a very favourable position. But for the sake of your study, although I do not like this, I feel I should tell you about a case in my extended family. One of my cousins married a second wife who already had three children. Shortly after this my cousin died in an accident. He died as a **kalāla**, he did not have children of his own, his father was dead. But he left two wives who would get 1/4 each, the rest was for his brothers and sisters. I can understand the second wife who produced a **waṣīya** in which her husband had bequeathed a considerable amount to her for the sake of her children. But the brothers and sisters went to court to contest the will. I am torn between two sides, I cannot say anything, but I am so very sorry that this should have happened."

"Did your cousin make the **waṣīya** because he had not arranged for the children to have the legal status of adopted children – for the purpose of being entitled to obligatory shares?"

"Yes, precisely. He had been married a very short time only, he was very attached to the second wife and cared for the children, but he hesitated to legalise them, so he preferred to make a will."

"But isn't this a case where a **waṣīya** would appear unobjectionable in every respect?"

"Theoretically speaking, yes. But my cousin's brothers insist that the children, who are all minors, should accept them as their guardians instead and thus keep the money in our family. You see, since the mother could not be their guardian, she would probably take a male from her family as guardian."

"And what do you expect will happen at court?"

"No-one knows. If she had addressed herself to a Qadi in the family he might have succeeded in talking her out of court proceedings. But with the new jurists who no

146 Goitein, 1970: No. 1110

longer receive their training at the mosque but go to all sorts of universities and have a lot of new ideas, anything is possible ..."

4.8.5 Muna: illiterate wife of a land owner, a rich heiress, "controls" family property inoffensively, example of a part-**munāsika**

Muna proved the most difficult person to find access to. She has a reputation of being withdrawn and is said to try and avoid meeting foreigners. It took several conversations with her husband before an interview could be arranged.

Muna is the illiterate wife of a well-established land owner, the son of a renowned Qadi. Both families own an impressive number of houses in Sana'a, including very valuable ones in the old city, and large plots of land outside Sana'a. She was married the "old way" as both she and her husband tell independently. The marriage was arranged between the two fathers who had also negotiated the transfer of land to take effect upon the death of Muna's father. The daughter had only seen her future husband through slits in curtains, and the man had only seen his future wife from a window while she had busied herself in the courtyard. Her **mahr** consisted of gold, dresses and cosmetics, all given to her at the time of marriage. She moved into her husband's house which belongs to him. When traffic in old Sana'a started to become "a nuisance" and tourists came in ever greater numbers, the husband decided to move to a quieter, healthier place and refurbished a house in Ar-Rawda, an ever more popular residential area between Sana'a and the Airport. It is an old house surrounded by vineyards, but equipped with the necessary conveniences to facilitate Muna's household duties. Her husband does all the shopping for the meals she prepares, Muna purchases what she wants for herself and the children. Although she shares an account with her husband at the bank, she asks her husband for any money she needs to do her shopping, and if she does not spend all of it keeps the rest and saves it in a cupboard. Whenever she needs to make a purchase, she asks for money again, and never touches what she has been saving.

"And how and why do you not run an account of your own?"

"When my father died, I inherited land and houses. The houses are let, and the land is used for agricultural purposes. All this brings money which is paid into the account under my name. My husband arranges and manages all this and he tells me about all the movements effected. As a matter of fact he also discusses with me all he does with his own plots of land, he converses with me and never takes a step without asking me what I think of it. You see, I am a very practical person, and I am sure my husband is pleased with this. When I got married people commented on the fact that I had been lucky to marry 'up the ladder'; my father had only been a merchant, but my husband's father was a Qadi. However, my father had been a very acute merchant and I learned a lot from him while still at home. I was not sent to school since this was not considered necessary, but I am not stupid. If anything happened to the men in our family I would know what to do and when to go to court. But as long as this is not necessary I prefer to stay at home. I know my husband likes to meet foreigners in Sana'a, partly because he rents our houses to them, partly because he likes to see their way of life. I do not like to meet them. There is nothing I could learn from them. I would not want to see my children imitate them. When my husband told me about you and insisted I should meet you I told him straight away that he could tell you what you want to know. But he kept telling me you do not want the information from him but from me personally. So I agreed to his inviting you for lunch. I never expected you not to stay in the **mafraj** with him after I had brought in the food and was surprised when you got up and followed into the kitchen. When you said you would not eat with my husband if I did not share the meal, and took the bread out of the oven yourself and talked to the children, I was at a loss what to do. When you told me about your grandchildren I felt I should be kind to you. It made me happy to see you enjoy my meal and eat it properly. When you insisted on helping me do the washing up and swept the floor I thought I must show you the other side of my life, the afternoon. This is why I dressed as I would have done for my Yemeni lady friends and am now sitting in the women's **mafraj** with you. I told my husband to pick you up by sunset and drive you home, as is becoming for a good woman."

And on the way back the obedient husband informed the guest that his wife had instructed him to explain to her a special case of **munāsiḵa** he had told her about, but that she had not really paid enough attention to at the time to be able to recall the entire story:

"Well, all this happened to a friend of mine. When his grandfather died, he left two wives, one with two sons and several daughters, the other with three sons and two daughters. The family did not have particularly good relations with either of the two wives. They agreed to make a part-**munāsiḵa**. They calculated the shares of the two women and their children and duly distributed the respective amounts while they agreed to leave the rest undivided."

"So that is a perfect example of women getting access to inheritance even before the men divide it up?"

"Yes, it would have been indeed. But for the fact that the women did not want to receive their shares. They only wanted to know how much it was and have a written paper stating their amounts. They preferred to leave the money with the family and only asked for the annual profits to be paid to them."

"And the men agreed to this?"

"They could not object. A **munāsik̲a** must be agreed upon by all parties concerned. And, my God, these women were clever, devilishly[147] clever. It is well known that any division of an estate will make the overall profits fall. Take the case of the greatest Yemeni industrial corporation, which is a family business. The man who manages the whole affair is immensely capable, headstrong and a character, and he dictates everything. So many members of the family have died but the division of inheritance is postponed time and again. Their **munāsik̲a** must comprise innumerable divisions by now – but everyone profits from not dividing, receiving annual money they could probably not make by investing their shares separately."

(And when the "example" of the above part-**munāsik̲a** was pointed out to a lawyer for his comment, the interviewer was told that as a matter of fact a number of lawyers had already been approached by members of the family to try and persuade the women to accept their shares, but that this had been to no avail.)

147 In this context surely a proverb should be referred to as found in Bowen, Donna Lee & Early, Evelyn A.: Everyday Life in the Muslim Middle East, 1993:78.

"The child of male sex comes to the world with sixty jnoun (spirits) in his body, the child of the female sex is born pure; but every year, the boy gets purified of a jinn, whereas the girl acquires one; and this is the reason that old women, sixty years and with sixty jnoun, are sorcerers more malignant than the devil himself. Blind she sews more material, lame she jumps over more rocks, deaf she knows all the news."

4.9 A Note on Respective Literature

Literature on interviews with women is abundant, and women researchers' contributions have started to appear in the East and the West. However, contributions on research of legal systems in the Middle East by women writers are much more sporadic, and if at all referring to the Yemen, they do not render comparable details of legal stipulatons vs actual practice in the context of inheritance, let alone specific interviews. The intricate aspects of inheritance are occasionally marginally referred to. For a comparison of specific inheritance interviews further studies would as yet have to be elaborated.

5. Conclusion

The documentation in Part One and the interviews in Part Two render a number of explanations and insight into the official rules and the inofficial practices of inheritance encountered in Sana'a.

The study was undertaken to render

- a test of actual practice vs normative patterns, and
- an account of conventional wisdom as applied by women.

The following summary is intended to explicitly draw the conclusions from the materials and narratives presented.

<u>The overall guidance of the Koran</u>

Samira recalls how her father insisted that all his children studied the Koran, and supervised them to make sure they understood the meaning, how he made them realise that they would always find guidance and explanation for every question. She also points out that where family relationships are intact, money or values may be passed on without any documents being drafted[148]. To divide justly in the best interest of the members of one's family is a religious law. The very idea of writing a will should be contemplated only if this is considered necessary to protect someone who might otherwise be disadvantaged. Yet, if you feel uneasy, a will is a must and you should not stay two nights without one under your pillow. By consulting the Koran as an encyclopaedia you are bound to find a solution and guidance on what to do, how to react. You will interpret Koranic verses differently in the course of your life, depending on your personal capabilities, learning, and experience.

<u>The behaviour expected of a good Muslim</u>

In every interview the subject of "a good Muslim" was mentioned or referred to at some point or other. Unfair treatment of other members of the family is agreed to

148 (and where there is abundant property to be passed on, perhaps also with a view to not disclosing the amounts involved)

be possible, but would entail deviating from the honourable path. A businessman who wishes to pass on his company to one particular son may resort to a fake transfer, selling it to a stranger who in turn sells it to the son without delay. Such a procedure would not leave Koranic heirs in any further bargaining position, but there is general agreement that this sort of "cleverness" is considered very "bad" (**ᶜaīb**)[149].

The truly haunting aspect appears to be the reaction of the good Muslim woman in the presence of not so good Muslim brothers. Zeinab was so ashamed when her brother tricked her out of her **mahr** that she refused to let anyone see this.

And the well-mannered behaviour of a good Muslim includes visiting the (extended) family. If he does not, this will not only create a bad impression of him, he also makes life awkward for those not visited. When Zeinab leads her annual sheep through the street she lives in, these are rare moments of sublime happiness for her.

<u>The importance of the presence of all heirs at any division procedure</u>

Whenever a division is made in the absence of heirs entitled to shares, this is in all probability done with the intention of arriving at some unfair settlement, detrimental to those absent. Since, in order to divide an estate, one person must be in charge of the procedure, this clearly involves complicity, the **wakīl** becomes an accessory to the crime.

Irrespective of the fact that such behaviour is incompatible with that of a good Muslim, the **wakīl** must surely be aware of the risk he runs of being made responsible once the damage is discovered. Here Zeinab's experience offers a prototype example of why this risk is taken. Whenever the loser is a woman she is intimidated by the threat of having to forego her right to go back to her family, and so far men can still rely on women not to take this risk, but rather, without demur, to allow themselves to be cheated.

---

149 **ᶜaīb** = shame, disgrace; a behaviour is considered shameful in the sense of "not honourable" as opposed to **ḥarām** = strictly forbidden and must be seen in the context of how much "honour" means

The **mahr** riddle

All the women interviewed point out that the way **mahr** is given or allotted, postponed or saved reflects the local or individual customs a particular family upholds. The respective articles in the latest version of Yemeni law provide the legal frame therefor, and the replies of the imams illustrate the variety of individual approaches possible and approved of.

The overriding importance of keeping the family property together

Aisha would not want her parents' house to become an object of sale. She willingly forgoes any money that might be due to her for the sake of always being able to go back home. She can do so much more easily than Zeinab, for whom even a small sum of money would have made all the difference in her daily life with her mother-in-law. But the underlying concept is the same for both.

In this context a passage from a recent publication by Leila Abu[150] should be referred to, as it emphasises the importance of keeping one's right to "a room":

"No woman sells her property, so tradition dictates. A woman has nothing but her husband and her property, and husbands cannot be trusted."

Aisha's husband gives his sister a plot of land he inherited but registers it under his name. The sister is married to someone from another family. If she were to die and the plot was hers, the husband from the other family would inherit part of it.

Munira's cousin did not legitimise the children his second wife brought with her when he married her. Upon his death his brothers want to become custodians since this implies they need not part with family property immediately, can perhaps try to find wives or husbands for the children in their own family. The widow, on the other hand, will prefer men from her own side so that property would be added to her family.

The apparent reluctance of women to insist on payment or transfer of their shares

Malika is fully aware she would be entitled to spend her mahr but prefers to save it for a future occasion. She was brought up by a dominating mother who made sure that she herself and her children were provided with the necessary means for a

150 Abouzeid, Leila: The Year of the Elephant, 1992:13

decent living. Malika is very lucky to have a husband who dearly loves her, she is very young and optimistic. She is looked after by people she can trust, and readily accepts their advice and "tutelage".

Muna and Munira, too, live in an environment of intact families. They receive all the money they ask for, they know that the family property is in the hands of wise members of their respective families, they have no understanding for any emancipatory aspirations.

Malika's mother makes another statement that may serve as a clue to actual inheritance patterns. "Can you see me ploughing my own fields?" Whether it is a field to plough, animals to herd, a company to run, usufruct of such an inheritance may prove problematic indeed. The woman would simply be unwise to even consider such a solution. Receiving annual contributions, even if the latter represent a reduced amount only, may very often be a fair settlement and bring much more than the woman could possibly have achieved herself.

An interesting contribution to this subject is offered by Moore[151] extrapolating that our understanding of women's control over property has to be considered in the light of the kinship relations in which the type of marriage concluded is embedded. Kinship systems help to "construct" women and men in different ways, as different sorts of persons, says Moore. Concepts of property are ultimately bound up with the concepts of the person.

Munāsika = a divine institution and a legal frame for any amount of interaction? or a perfidious instrument for withholding shares?

Malika's mother-in-law knew that there had been an agreement to postpone the division of inheritance when her grandfather died. She only learnt much later that she had subsequently been cheated by her brothers. She was a mature woman when she made the discovery, she had established her position in the family. She was aware that going to court was the only possible remedy and that she could only win. If the court turned down her complaint she would not be worse off than before, would not lose any position or endanger an inter-family arrangement. This attitude should also be seen as evidence of women's emancipation, as a practical example for the new spirit slowly but undeniably manifesting itself.

151 Moore, H.: Feminism and Anthropology, 1988, Chapter 3:71

The family of Muna's husband's friend hoped to disengage themselves from females they would have preferred to pay off. But the women fully realised that they would be better off to vote for regular distribution of profits than if they accepted a single lump sum. And they could afford to behave in such a manner, they were widows, fairly advanced in years – which in the Arab world always demands respect – and sufficiently well off to be obstinate and have a say in matters.

The position the two women will be in for perhaps a number of years is a repeatable experience – to apply laboratory terminology in testing. Many women approached on this subject in Sana'a admitted to receiving annual payments relating to a postponed division of inheritance. Unless earmarked specifically as such, the respective payments will not even appear as inheritance in any statistics, even if compiled, and less so as proof of women's regular income, since by far the majority of such women are not "gainfully employed".

****

It is hoped that the material presented and the considerations undertaken justify the overall conclusion drawn which surely should be to state that women in Sana'a do inherit but very often in a way not in line with official prescriptions. The study sheds light on the normative role law exerts, as it does in any other complex society. Legal provisions permit a fair amount of interpretation. Actual practice incorporates a number of aspects imbedded in customary law.

There is one more aspect requiring special reference. Part Two of the study may well be questioned as not statistically representative. The majority of women interviewed belong to "better families". But it would have been futile to interview women who cannot inherit because there is nothing to pass on. The standards adhered to in a society are established by those materially in a position to do so. A similar pattern is to be found in this respect also in the West.

The example quoted as evidence of women's economic independence should perhaps be referred to again too. Five percent may appear a very small percentage, but, as was pointed out, this figure refers to the number of bank accounts in the name of women. No figures are available for the number of accounts held by women together with men. Perhaps a comparative investigation of the respective situations in Yemen and in a Western country would bring surprising results, approximating Sana'ani habits?

As far as inheritance is concerned, it remains to be debated whether some of the forms of passing on values/property can still be termed inheritance, and also for how long this system, as encountered, will remain practicable in the light of rapidly changing circumstances.

Katabat Anisa al-nemsawīya

6. Bibliography

ᶜAbd al ᶜAtī, Hammūdah:
1977 The Family Structure in Islam
American Trust Publication, Indianapolis

Abouzeid, Leila:
1992 Year of the Elephant
The American University in Cairo Press, Cairo

Ahmed, Leila:
1993 Women and Gender in Islam
The American University in Cairo Press, Cairo

Al-Azmah, Aziz:
1993 Ibn Khaldūn
The American University in Cairo Press, Cairo

Al-Bāschā, A.Y.:
1987 Frauen im Jemen einst und heute
in: W. Daum, Ed. JEMEN
Innsbruck/Frankfurt a.M.

Al-Hubaishi, H.A.:
1988 Legal System and Basic Law in Yemen
SPHINX PUBLISHING, London

Altorki, Soraya:
1986 Women in Saudi-Arabia, Ideology and Behaviour among the Elite
New York Columbia University Press, New York

Altorki, Soraya
& El Solh, Camilla Fawzi:
1988 Arab Women in the Field
Syracuse University Press, New York

Amin, S.H.:
1985 Middle East Legal Systems
Royston Limited, Glasgow

Beck, L. & Keddie, N.:
1978 Women in the Muslim World
Harvard University Press, Cambridge

Bergsträsser, N:
1935 Grundzüge des Islamischen Rechts,
bearbeitet und herausgegeben von Joseph Schacht
Verlag von Walter de Gruyter & Co,
Berlin und Leipzig

Bourdieu, Pierre:
1972 Esquisse d'une théorie de la pratique, précédé de trois études d'éthnologie kabyle
Geneva

Buringa, Joke:
1992 Bibliography on Women in Yemen
Ed. Marta Colburn
American Institute for Yemeni Studies,
Westbury, New York

Bowen, Donna Lee & Early, Evelyn A.:
1993 Everyday life in the Muslim Middle East
Indiana University Press, Bloomington and Indianapolis

Bruck, Gabriele vom:
1987 Re-Defining Identity: Women in San'a
in; W. Daum, Ed. JEMEN:396bis
Innsbruck/Frankfurt a.M.

1991 Descent and Religious Knowledge:
Houses of Learning in Modern San'a
Thesis submitted to LSE, London

Chelhod, Joseph:
1975 La Société Yéménite et le Droit
in: L'Homme, avr.-juin, XV (2) pp.67-86, Paris

Coulson N.J.:
1964 A History of Islamic Law
Edinburgh
1969 Conflicts and Tensions in Islamic Jurisprudence
The University of Chicago Press,
Chicago and London

Coulson, Noel & Hinchcliffe, Doreen:
1970 Women and Law Reform in Contemporary Islam
in: Beck, C. & Keddie, N.: Women in the Muslim World,
Cambridge and Harvard University Press, Cambridge/Mass.

Delcambre, Anne Marie:
1987 Mahomet, La parole d'Allah
Editions Gallimard, Paris

Deonna, Laurence:
1983 Yémen
Les Editions Arthaud, Paris

Dorsky, Susan:
1986 Women of ᶜAmran
A Middle Eastern Ethnographic Study
University of Utah Press, Salt Lake City

Fayein, Claudie
1990 Vies de femmes au Yémen, Récits de Nagiba,
L'Harmattan, Paris

Frese-Weghöft, Gisela:
1986 Ein Leben in der Unsichtbarkeit
Frauen im Jemen
Rowohlt, Hamburg

Gerholm, Tomas:
1988 Aspects of Inheritance in North Yemen
in: Ann Elizabeth Mayer (ed.)
Property, Social Structure and Law in the Modern Midd le East
Albany, State University of New York Press, N.Y.

Gingrich, André:
1989 Der Agrarkalender der Munebbih
Habilitationsschrift Universität Wien

1989 Review on: S.H. Amin: Law and justice in contemporary Yemen, Glasgow 1987
in: ORIENT, German Journal for Politics and Economics of the Middle East
30. Jahrgang Nr. 2:290
Leske Verlag + Budrich GmbH, Opladen

Girtler, Roland:
1976 Rechtssoziologie - Thesen und Möglichkeiten
(Das "Sein" und das "Sollen")
Wilhelm Fink Verlag, München

Goitein, S.D.F.:
1979 Jemenica
Sprichwörter und Redensarten aus Zentral-Jemen
E.J. Brill, Leiden

Graham, Helga:
1978 The Arabian Time Machine
Heinemann, London

Haeri, Shaykh Fadhlalla:
1993 The Elements of Islam
Zahra Trust Publications
Element Books Ltd., Shaftsbury, Dorset

Harris, Marvin:
1985 The Sacred Cow and the Abominable Pig
Simon and Schuster, New York

Hartmann, Richard:
1944 Die Religion des Islam
Verlag von E.S. Mittler & Sohn, Berlin

Hjärpe, Jan:
1983 Islamic Fundamentalism and Women
in: Studies on Asian Topics No. 6
Bo Utas, Curzon Press, London and Malmö

Hoebel, E.A.:
1964 The Law of Primitive Men
Cambridge/Mass.

Johnson, Catherine;
1992 ICD's Contribution on Women's Legal Rights,
Leiden

Juynboll; Th.W.:
1910 Handbuch des Islamischen Gesetzes nach der Lehre der schafi'itischen Schule
Otto Harrassowitz, Leipzig

Kielstra, Niko:
1885 Women in Islam
in: Gellner, E.: Islamic Dilemmas
Mouton de Gruyter, Hawthorne, N.Y

Lèvi-Strauss, Claude:
1958 Anthropologie Structurale
Librairie Plon, Paris

Lewcock, R. & Serjeant, R.B.:
1983 Sana'a - An Arabian Islamic City, World of Islam
Festival Trust Publication, London

Madelung, Wilferd:
1965 Der Imām al-Qāsim ibn Ibrāhīm und die Glaubenslehre der Zayditen
Berlin

1979 Shi^{c}i Attitudes Towards Women as Reflected in Fiqh
in: A. Lutfi (Ed): Society and the Sexes in Medieval Islam, Malibu

Makhlouf, Carla:
1979 Changing Veils: Women and Modernisation in North Yemen
Croom Helm, London

Malti Douglas, Fedwa:
1992 Woman's Body - Woman's Word
The American University in Cairo Press, Cairo

Mansour, Fahmy:
1913 La condition de la femme dans la tradition et l'évaluation de l'islamisme
Librairie Félix Alcan, Paris

Meissner, Jeffrey A.:
1987 Tribes at the Core: Legitimacy, Structure and Power in Zaydi Yemen
UMI Michigan

Meriwether, Margaret L.:
1993 Women's Property
in: Arab Woman, ed. by Tucker, Judith E., Indiana University Press, Bloomington and Indianapolis

Mernissi, Fatima:
1090 Sultanes oubliées, Femmes Chefs d'Etat en Islam
Editions Albin Michel, Paris

Moore, H.:
1988 Feminism and Anthropology
University of Minnesota Press, Minnesota

Morris, Timothy:
1991 The Despairing Developer, Diary of an Aid Worker in the Middle East
I.B.Tauris & Co Ltd, London & New York

Mundy, Martha:
1976 Women's Inheritance in Highland Yemen
in: Arabian Studies V:161-187
1988 Islamic Law
ed. Aziz al-Azmeh, Routledge, London & New York

Murphy, R.F. and Kasdan, L.:
1959 The Structure of Parallel Cousin Marriage
in: American Anthropologist, ed. Walter Goldschmidt, Vol. 61
Menasha, Wisconsin

Musil, Alois:
1928 The manners and customs of the Rwala Bedouins
in Oriental Exploration and Studies No. 6
American Geographical Society, New York

Myntti, Cynthia:
1979 Women and Development in Yemen Arab Republic GTZ
publication, Eschborn

Mutahhari, Murtada:
1981 The Rights of Women in Islam
WOFIS, Teheran

Nicolaison, Ida:
1983 Introduction to "Women in Islamic Societies"
in: Studies on Asian Topics No. 6
Bo Utas, Curzon Press, London & Malmö

Niebuhr, Carsten:
1773 Travel to Arabia
J. Mueller, Copenhagen

Nippa, Annegret:
1991 Haus und Familie in arabischen Ländern: Vom Mittelalter bis
zur Gegenwart
Beck's Archäologische Bibliothek, München

Sahlins, Marshall:
1976 Culture and Practical Reason
The University of Chicago, Chicago

Smith, Jane I.:
1980 Women in Contemporary Muslim Societies
Associated University Press Inc., London

Schacht, Josef:
1989 An Introduction to Islamic Law
Oxford University Press, Oxford

Stark, Freya:
1973 Winter in Arabia
Overlook Press, N.Y.

Stiegner, Roswitha G.:
1989 Die Stellung der Frau in Altsüdarabien
"Jemen, Im Land der Königin von Saba": 80
Ausstellungskatalog Museum für Völkerkunde, Wien

Strehl, Franz:
1989 Reformarbeit in bürokratischen Organisationen: Entscheidungsprozesse und ihre organisatorische Gestaltung als Grundlage von Reformprojekten,
Baden-Baden

Strohtmann, R.:
1912 Das Staatsrecht der Zaiditen
Verlag von Karl J. Trübner, Strassburg

Thesiger, Wilfred:
1959 Travel through the Empty Quarter
Longmans Green, London

Tucker, Judith E.:
1993 Arab Women
Indiana University Press, Bloomington and Indianapolis

ur-Rahman, Tanzil:
1980 A Code of Muslim Personal Law, Vol. II
Islamic Publishers, Pakistan

Walters, Delores M:
1987 Perceptions of Social Inequality in the Yemen Arab Republic,
UMI Dissertation Service, Michigan

Zabarah, Mohammad Ahmad:
1988 Yemen - Traditionalism vs Modernity
Praeger Special Studies
Praeger Publication, Greenwood

*****

Arab authors in Arabic

Al-Hanbali, Mohammad Said:
1985 Uṣūl ᶜilm al-mawārīt
dar al-kitāb al-ᶜilmīya, Beirut

Daradka, Yasin Ahmad Ibrahim:
1983 al-mīrāt fī-š-šarᶜaīa al-islāmīya
dar al-aḥkām, Amman

ᶜAbdulwali, Mohammad Ahmad:
1986 ṣanᶜā'- madīna maftūḥa
dar al-awda, Sana'a

*****

Dictionaries used and Encyclopaedias and reference material consulted:

Encyclopaedia Britannica
1988 Encyclopaedia Britannica, Inc.,
The University of Chicago
(I:508-10)

Grand Dictionnaire Larousse Encyclopédique
1985 Librairie Larousse, Paris
(Vol. 10:10965-69)

Encyclopaedia Universalis
1985 Encyclopaedia Universalis S.A., Paris
(Corpus 18:1145-51)

Journal of the Economic and Social History of the Orient - 28/1975:53-114 (Judicial Records) - Faculty of Law, Sana'a University

Yemen Constitution: Draft Constitution of the State of Unified Yemen, by
Carol Tenney & David W. Mc Clintock
Ocean Publications, Inc., Dobbs Ferry, N.Y.
1990 in: Constitutions of the Countries of the World
Editors: Albert P. Blaustein & Gisbert H. Flanz

Official Gazette of Republic of Yemen No. 3/1992
(al-jarīda al-rasmīya: al-qarār al-jumhūrī bi-l-qānūn,
qānūn ahwāl aš-šaksīya
raqm 20)

Official Gazette of Democratic People's Republic of Yemen No. 1/1974
(qānūn al-usra)

Bell, Richard:
1960 The Translation of the Qur'ān
T & T Clark, Edinburgh

Cahen, Claude:
1987 Der Islam I
Fischer Taschenbuchverlag, Frankfurt am Main

Denffer, Ahmed von : Herausgeber
1984 "Allahs Gesandter hat gesagt ...", Auswahl und Übersetzung
Eva und Omar Al-Shabassy und Armin Walters
Publikation des Islam, Lüzelbach

Glasse, Cyril:
1989 The Concise Encyclopedia of Islam
Harper, San Francisco

Grunebaum, G.E. v.: Herausgeber
1971 Der Islam II
Fischer Taschenbuchverlag, Frankfurt am Main

Wehr, Hans:
1979 A Dictionary of Modern Written Arabic
Fourth Edition, Otto Harrassowitz, Wiesbaden

no author A Dictionary of English and Arabic Proverbs
1987 The Adornment of Speech
Dar-al-Bihar, Beirut

Abu Harb, Mohammad Hair:
1985 al-mu^{c}jam al-madrasī
Published by Ministry of Education, Damaskus

Imam Yahya b. al-Husayn:
1407 a.h. kitāb al-aḥkām fī bayān al-halāl wa-l-ḥarām
Library of Old University, Sana'a

Imam al-Murtafa':
šarh al-azhār
1341 a.h. Vol.3
1342 a.h. Vol.4
Library of Old University, Sana'a

Al-Maridi, Yahya Ahmad b.:
no date al baḥr az-zājar
Vol. 6
Library of Old University, Sana'a

Kolibri 360 GmbH
Ferdinand-Jühlke-Straße 7
99095 Erfurt, Deutschland
produktsicherheit@kolibri360.de